RESEARCH FACILITIES OF THE FUTURE

ANNALS OF THE NEW YORK ACADEMY OF SCIENCES
Volume 735

RESEARCH FACILITIES OF THE FUTURE

Edited by Stanley Stark

The New York Academy of Sciences
New York, New York
1994

The cover art is a reproduction of a construction by Joseph Cornell entitled *Soap Bubble Set*, courtesy of the Wadsworth Atheneum, Hartford. Purchased through the Gift of Henry and Walter Keney.

Library of Congress Cataloging-in Publication Data

Research facilities of the future / edited by Stanley Stark.
      p.   cm. — (Annals of the New York Academy of Sciences; v. 735)
    Includes bibliographical references and index.
    ISBN 0-89766-903-7 (alk. paper). — ISBN 0-89766-904-5 (pbk. : alk. paper)
    1. Research institutes—Management—Congresses. I. Stark. Stanley. II. Series.
    Q11.N5   vol. 735
    [Q180.57]
    500 s—dc20
    [727'.5]   94-28061
                                     CIP

PCP
Printed in the United States of America
ISBN 0-89766-903-7 (cloth)
ISBN 0-89766-904-5 (paper)
ISSN 0077-8923

ANNALS OF THE NEW YORK ACADEMY OF SCIENCES

Volume 735

August 31, 1994

RESEARCH FACILITIES OF THE FUTURE [a]

Editor

STANLEY STARK

Workshop Organizers

STANLEY STARK AND JEFFREY S. FRENCH

CONTENTS

[a] This volume is the result of a meeting entitled Preparing for the Research Facilities of the Future:
A Collaborative Workshop held on June 16-17, 1993 in New York, New York and sponsored by
the New York Academy of Sciences.

The Future Outlook

Financial assistance was received from:

Supporters
- LEHRER MCGOVERN BOVIS OF NEW JERSEY INC.
- MORSE DIESEL INTERNATIONAL

Contributors
- SORDONI SKANSKA CONSTRUCTION CO.
- GENERAL ELECTRIC FOUNDATION
- HOFFMANN-LA ROCHE INC.
- HAINES LUNDBERG WAEHLER

Opening Remarks

RODNEY W. NICHOLS

The New York Academy of Sciences
2 East 63rd Street
New York, New York 10021

Welcome to our meeting. I particularly want to thank Stanley Stark and Jeffrey French for putting the meeting together. We also appreciate the efforts of a long-time leader in the Academy's programs, Morris Shamos, for his astute guidance and planning.

TRENDS IN THE LABORATORY ENVIRONMENT

George Brown, the Chairman of the House Committee on Space, Science and Technology, was here a few months ago and opened his talk with an inversion of an old aphorism. He said, "invention is the mother of necessity." That's true for much of what we are doing in lab construction and renovation.

For example, having had experience working in labs and with building and renovating them, I know that advanced instruments create new ways of thinking about what is required in the lab environment's space, traffic patterns, and supporting resources. Furthermore, given the high costs of facilities and the needs for multiple assets of interdisciplinary expertise, larger groups–in fields ranging from high-energy physics to molecular biology–are essential for sharing equipment and tackling tough research questions. This is true, of course, for big science; but middle-sized science and little science also require much more interaction among bench investigators. Another well-documented trend is the growth in new sets of regulatory requirements (e.g., storing chemicals, and dealing with animals). All of this means that what it takes to plan a research facility necessitates more communication and fresh design approaches among the concerned parties.

These trends put the lie to the remark that I understand Phillip Johnson once made. He was reputed to have said that "architecture is the art of how to waste space." We no longer have the aesthetic notion of an architect just being asked to give us a pretty building, although excellence in design always enhances morale and productivity. Certainly, architecture today is the art of how to wring the most productive space out of a crowded, high-technology setting that needs superb communications among teams.

The subject of this workshop is important for at least four reasons. I will take a moment on each. First, it is nationally important. Second, increasingly

1

it is becoming internationally relevant. Third, it is comparatively novel for the New York Academy of Sciences. And finally, it is critical for the New York region.

NATIONAL ISSUES

It is nationally important for a whole series of reasons. One is the growth over the recent years in what is called "earmarking" of money by Congress for facilities. The total amount of earmarking for research and development facilities funding in fiscal year (FY92) was $150 million for university campuses. Most were not peer reviewed, and there are grave questions about the quality of some projects. Yet because we are talking about major investments, it is crucial that whatever happens with the money be efficient and productive. Research universities have great stresses in obtaining the capital to modernize their facilities. There is a market for getting better knowledge about how to maximize the utility of every dollar universities can muster.

Other national considerations include the "national labs," presently undergoing major "conversion." I do not think any of us are quite sure how this conversion process will pan out, but we know that the uses of laboratories will change. Furthermore, corporate research and development labs are, after a major period of building, pausing for various reasons; yet renovations no doubt will continue. And then of course we have big science, such as the ill-fated Super Conducting Super Collider, for which reliable construction cost estimates became the key issue.

Even "minor" changes in the federal investment (perhaps only a few tens of millions of dollars) are important not only to the people working there, but also to the public's perception of how well R&D funding is used. The history here is interesting and is beyond the scope of my time today. Suffice it to say that the federal government has been the sponsor of major labs of all kinds over several decades – from material sciences and engineering, to the National Institutes of Health's support of facilities all over the country, to the archipelago of Department of Energy labs. For the future, there is much anxiety about whether we will have the capital for modernization, and whether the available capital will be used well.

INTERNATIONAL SIGNIFICANCE

On the international side, many of you know the markets better than I. A key projection is that during the 1990s, there will be many new research and development facilities built in the so-called Third World. As Third World countries modernize and industrialize, which they are, as they build their capacity for scientists and engineers, which they are, as they see that a critical path to prosperity is world trade, which they do, they are going to be constructing R&D facilities. There are ample data to support this outlook from UNESCO, the World Bank, the OECD (Organization for Economic Cooperation and Development), and others.

In North America, as I have recently documented in an essay with Tom Ratchford on "North American Science and Technology" for UNESCO's *World Science Report 1993*, funding is under heavy pressure. In Canada, for example, as in the United States, the challenge is to find the capital to modernize facilities that were first class, but are now obsolescent. In Mexico, with a booming economy, funding for science has been growing by 20% a year since 1988. It went through a severe trough in the mid-1980s when the price of oil dropped. But it has more than recovered from the early 1980s, and major facilities probably will be built in Mexico over the rest of the decade.

For the New York Academy of Sciences—with one-third of our nearly 40,000 members outside the United States—this workshop is going to be of interest to many of our members, mostly working scientists and engineers, wherever they are. Engaging our global membership on problems of common interest is our highest priority. So this meeting on R&D facilities fits perfectly into our goal to recognize and serve our global supporters.

POLICY ISSUES AND INTERDISCIPLINARY NOVELTY

Which leads to my third point: this is a somewhat novel conference for the Academy. It is more interdisciplinary than many of our meetings, and it includes people from many more professional backgrounds. It is certainly more policy oriented and resource oriented than many of our specialized scientific research meetings.

Perhaps most important, the workshop has extensive representation from industry, which, frankly, is essential. About three-fourths of the million or so scientists and engineers in the United States who work in R&D are employed in industry. While this Academy in the distant past thought of itself largely as a surrogate of the university, today it is not, and cannot be, merely "academic." This is an academy of science (and engineering), and that means we must enlist more of the scientists, engineers, and research physicians who work in industry and government. We intend to pursue that goal in the future, and in the year I have been here I have encouraged this kind of meeting as one of the ways to exercise our intersectoral reach.

NEW YORK'S NEEDS AND OPPORTUNITIES

Let me close with obvious reminders about why this meeting is important to the New York area. We have many firms that conduct large-scale, world-class R&D in every field–including an extraordinary ensemble of world-class biomedical research centers.

We are also a center of telecommunications. This subject may not be on the agenda in an explicit way. But modern telecommunications, and the impacts of the information revolution noted in some abstracts, clearly influence how science is done and how individual investigators communicate. This will have many rippling effects on the way we think about how to design labs.

Another example is biotechnology. The New York City Mayor and the Deputy Mayor for Economic Development aim to foster the growth of biotech firms. Those firms are going to build facilities, and/or renovate them. So New York, as a center of biomedical science, which it is, needs the "highest and best" facilities, along with other ingredients of a healthy business climate, to encourage biotechnology.

This meeting, bringing together the people in New York and elsewhere who care about design for R&D, ought to help the City and the metropolitan area chart the future. A key question will be whether developments such as Metrotech in Brooklyn are what we envision. Is greater centralization a more effective way to improve communications, and a more efficient use of regulatory staffs and supporting resources such as shared facilities? So are we going to see further consolidation and centralization of facilities in New York? Or, are we going to lack capital so that institutions are forced to an opposite vision: a highly decentralized view of labs where activity will be limited to a few thousand square feet here (or a few floors there) and only rarely the construction of a major new laboratory building. If capital remains scarce, this latter vision may prevail, not only in New York but throughout much of the country. The design challenges in these two viewpoints would be different, and the cost effectiveness calculations would be demanding.

THE CHALLENGE

Too often, a facility's design is taken for granted. Yet the "supportive environment" for research is critical for productivity, as more working scientists and research executives recognize. Your challenge is to show how the lessons learned from experience in the past, and how the moving frontier in both science and other features of the research environment for the future, can bring new satisfaction and efficiency to our facilities.

Introduction and Conference Overview

STANLEY STARK

Haines Lundberg Waehler
115 Fifth Avenue
New York, New York 10003

PURPOSE OF THE WORKSHOP

The scientific enterprise is a major force within our society and our economy. It represents nearly $150 billion in annual expenditures, it accounts for 2.7% of our GDP, and it employs approximately 950,000 scientists and engineers. The research lab, the entire facility itself, is the primary resource of experimental science. It is critical that we assure that the major investment in this resource can accommodate the future needs of science as we project forward.

We step into the future every day. But as the year 2000 approaches, our attention is particularly focused because we will be crossing a threshold that defines now from then.

The purpose of the two-day Workshop was to develop some forward vision that would allow us to anticipate the future and how to provide for it in our research facilities. The Workshop offered us the opportunity to escape from the tyranny of the urgent. The mission was to examine what the research facilities of the future would be as they both respond to the shifting forces that shape science and as they anticipate the changes to come. Our ambition was that upon leaving the Workshop, the audience and participants would all have developed the sensitivity that would allow us to adapt to future conditions, or at least confront them, in a thoughtful and intelligent manner.

This topic was and is too broad and deep to be represented by any single constituency. That is why the Workshop was collaborative, involving 16 speakers and a participatory audience from the realms of science, research management, scientific journalism, architecture, engineering, construction, universities, corporations, and government agencies. Everyone illuminated a different facet of the topic. One of the major outcomes of this gathering was the diversity of viewpoints.

Considering the nature of the future is to hypothesize incipient change. Most change is incremental, gradual, more of the same, but to a greater or lesser degree. Some change is sudden and abrupt, without precedent. The recent emergence of a global village, powered by telecommunications and computer capability 30 years after Marshall McLuhan postulated it, is a change the elements of which developed incrementally, but now has erupted with dramatic suddenness in ways that have startled us.

Many of the speakers approached changes in an incremental manner. Others had forecast some non sequiturs, changes or responses that are sudden and dramatic in direction.

The Workshop was structured to examine the issues through a cycle of expert presentations offering a diversity of views, roundtable discussions, and audience question and answer sessions. Day 1 was devoted to the forecasts of the research community followed by the design community's discussion of how facilities are currently anticipating the future. Day 2 concentrated on the future itself. We entertained speculations about what the lab(s) of the future might actually be. Finally, we focused on a specific case–considerations of future reuse of Federal labs.

Scientists want more space, predictable environments, fewer obstacles posed by the facilities themselves, and autonomy. On the other hand, research managers, both corporate and academic, believe the scientific community will have to do more with less. And, they will have to do it more quickly. Research facility designers will have to cope with conflicting pressures both from within the scientific community and increasingly from society at large to design flexible, broadly responsive, and cost-effective facilities. And they will have to find new ways to resolve the conflict between the rapid and frequent changes in science and technology and the static nature of buildings and building systems.

Dr. Nathaniel Heintz, Rockefeller University, and Samuel Williamson, New York University, made clear that scientists expect to be more entrepreneurial, more mobile, and will conduct science in a variety of settings, such as small-scale research centers where they will have their own firms to maintain control over their research. The lab will continue to be the heart of the scientific workplace, requiring more adaptability, more user autonomy, and tighter control over the environment to match the growing sensitivity of the equipment. More changes can be expected in the support space environment than within the lab proper. Because labs are where scientists live as much as where they work, there are higher expectations of the quality of design. More concessions to user comfort will be demanded and a reduction of barriers between disciplines. Amenity, communication, interaction are considered as important as the technical aspects of labs.

Both felt that the lab must be regarded as a facility that operates around the clock that would require greater concessions to personal security and would increase the ability of scientists to get around via more and friendlier stairways. They regarded elevators as particular obstacles to effective use of their time.

As a biologist, Dr. Heintz viewed the lab as both a work space and a living space. He had high expectations of user friendliness (light, warm finishes, spaces to sit and write). As a physicist, Dr. Williamson regarded the lab more as a workshop in which equipment and apparatus could be reconfigured easily. Walls, ceilings, and floors were regarded as obstacles. But he did not regard the lab as a living space. That status was reserved for his office.

Steven Cohen, Yale University Medical Center, stressed that universities are constrained by capital and limited by the government in recouping their investment. Societal returns are high, but capital returns are low. The result will be smaller projects, mostly renovations, phased over longer periods of time. While the overall stock of academic research space is adequate, it is not reasonably distributed, nor are there sophisticated tools available to measure rates of return on physical capital or to define the capital costs attributable to a project. These tools must be developed if these investment decisions are to be made more accurately.

Dr. Leon Lewis, Hoffmann-La Roche, saw competition, market, and governmental pressure leading to lower research and development investment by pharmaceutical companies affecting corporate, academic, and philanthropically sponsored research. The pressures on future facilities will be toward higher population densities and lower occupancy and construction costs, while maintaining flexibility, functional effectiveness, attractiveness to younger scientists, and more control over operating costs.

In discussing how the design community is currently designing the future into research facilities, Robert McGhee, Howard Hughes Medical Institute, stressed that lab building utilization must be tested in terms of 5 to 10 years after initial occupancy. The biggest source of change has been the increasing sophistication and quantity of equipment, which demands more service in labs and more specialized support space for equipment accommodation.

Leevi Kiil, Haines Lundberg Waehler, Architects, Engineers, and Planners, emphasized facility endurance via flexible building mechanical system distribution pathways that allow modification and change: central vertical shafts, utility corridors, interstitial floors. Distribution patterns must mesh with the mandates for flexibility and communication as shaped by organizational culture. The access to the facility's infrastructure both to maintain and to modify is a prerequisite capability to accommodate the future.

Timothy Baker, R.G. Vanderweil Engineers, stressed that state-of-the-art mechanical, electrical, and plumbing systems are increasing the control researchers and facility managers have over their lab environments while reducing energy consumption. But maintenance and operations staffs must become attuned to running these sophisticated systems if their benefits are to be realized.

Dr. Leon Lewis indicated that strategic planning is evolving toward a total quality management (TQM) approach that assesses facilities as being more focused on supporting the organization's overall research mission and is less targeted on the needs of individual scientists.

Although the future has not arrived yet, our discussions speculated on the actual forms the labs of the future might take. Conference coproponent, architect Jeffrey French of Ballinger, proposed that the options for differing mixes on the lab floors between lab offices and support spaces are the critical areas where the future will be shaped. The ability to change this mix quickly, in synch with the pace and character of research, will be the prime attribute of flexibility. Tim Baker stressed the drive toward "green" buildings. That is, buildings whose systems conserve energy, are nonpolluting, and produce or pass through minimal or no waste.

I discussed factors such as the pressure to push people out of the labs and how that might make buildings wider as people move to the exterior and labs move deeper toward the center of the lab floor. Explorations of options for flexibility included shell labs (raw space, not fit-out but with infrastructure); anchor-bridge arrangements (clusters of customized specific support space flanked by general loftlike space); and portable, self-contained environments that can be wheeled into a space and plugged in for service delivery. The fact that the scientific community is growing younger suggests that we will be called upon to inject more play into the research environment. At the very least, they will expect more out of their working environments. Other future possibilities offered include the demand for environmentally benign systems, global communications systems, R&D buildings as real estate commodities, and the movement of R&D facilities back to the urban industrial fringe in response to increasingly restrictive demands imposed by suburban communities, e.g., restrictions on height, use, site coverage, and parking.

Christopher Hill, of the RAND Corp.'s Critical Technologies Institute, reported on the uncertain outlook for the Federal laboratories: the scramble to find fundable new missions, the emphasis on collaborative ventures with industry, the overall decline in federal funding, new initiatives in Congress to restructure the Federal research effort.

The audience was an active and informed participant in all of these discussions. Together with the panelists, they shared a general resolution to reconsider the ground rules governing research facility design: planning, flexibility, the relationship between facility obsolescence and cost, and facility management.

Most importantly, a consensus was reached to continue these discussions with peers and colleagues because, although we cannot predict, it is our responsibility to anticipate. And anticipation requires continuous scrutiny and reevaluation.

ACKNOWLEDGMENTS

As Proponents of the Workshop, we would like to acknowledge and credit the following individuals without whose participation and support neither the Workshop nor the *Annal* could have been realized:

- **New York Academy Of Sciences:**
  Rodney Nichols, Chief Executive Officer
  Dr. Morris Shamos, President Emeritus and Member of the Conference Committee
  Dr. Victor Wouk, Member, Conference Committee
  Geraldine Bussacco, Conference Director
  Ann Collins, Communications Director
  Bill Boland, Executive Editor, *The Annals*
  Sheila Kane, Editorial Staff, *The Annals*

- **Supporters, Who Provided Major Funding to Conduct the Workshop:**
  Lehrer McGovern Bovis, and Norberte Young, Exec. VP, who participated in Workshop Panels.
  Morse Diesel International, and both Peter McGee, Director and Anthony Winson, VP, who participated in Workshop Panels.

- **Contributors, Who Provided Additional Funding to Conduct the Workshop:**
  Sordoni Skanska Construction Co.
  The G. E. Foundation

- **Staff at Haines Lundberg Waehler:**
  Jane Cohn, Director of Public Relations
  Kent Holliday, Architect
  June Cardile and Bridget Means, Graphics Staff
  Frances Nolan, Administrative Assistant to Mr. Stark

- **And, the Speakers and Participants.**

Stanley Stark
Jeffrey French

Future Trends Affecting the Lab

The Life Scientist's View

NATHANIEL HEINTZ

Howard Hughes Medical Institute
The Rockefeller University
1230 York Avenue, Box 260
New York, New York 10021-6399

I am both a Professor of Molecular Biology at Rockefeller University and an Investigator of the Howard Hughes Institute. I occupy laboratory space in a beautiful new building at Rockefeller (the Rockefeller Research Tower). My task is to give some impressions about life as a scientist and what is important to scientists in terms of the laboratory itself and the buildings that we inhabit.

It is probably not generally appreciated that science is extremely competitive and that the top investigators have essentially unlimited mobility in the field. For people to move between universities is not regarded negatively. This mobility has a very strong impact on science because the quality of the facilities and the type of laboratory you inhabit will basically have a very large effect on which university you choose to do your research in. So it is true that universities that design and have available absolutely first-class laboratory space will be the ones that attract the top investigators and produce the best science.

I believe that this has always been true. Right now it is more significant because there are many universities that are building facilities and the mobility between universities is increasing. That is particularly important because communication between scientists has become much easier. With all of the electronic means available to communicate to your favorite colleague, communication no longer requires that you have to be next door. It was quite different 30 years ago when, if you wanted to work with someone, you had to be in the laboratory next door, or at least at the same university. So that puts pressure on the universities to design first-class laboratories with state-of-the-art capabilities to attract the best investigators.

My next general point is that science is a very unorganized pursuit. People work long hours that are quite variable; laboratories function around the clock. This has several impacts. The first is that the laboratories should *not* be looked at as someplace where people simply work. The number of hours that people in training put in the laboratory is much greater than the time they spend anywhere else, so it really needs to be a pleasant place for them.

That is translated into having, for example, good lighting, nice windows, and a view of the outside so you do not feel like a lab animal when you are trying to do your experiments. And I think that the idea is certainly borne out in our new building. Very large windows are in the laboratory, and the views they afford of the Manhattan skyline and the East River are an important asset. People love to work in the new building. Buildings that, for some reason that I do not understand, have corridors on the outside and the scientists themselves squirreled away in little labs in the interior are not going to attract the best scientists.

Because of the amount of time spent in the lab and the variable hours of the people working in the labs, security is extremely important. Each building must have the flexibility and the security systems available so that people working at 2 or 3 in the morning feel secure and feel like there is something actually happening around them, that they are not in a void. This is particularly true in large metropolitan areas. It is nerve wracking for most of us, but especially for women working in the laboratory late at night, to see someone they do not know walking through the building. So security should be addressed not as just a required utility system in the life of a university, but as a significant and positive investment that makes people feel comfortable in the laboratory. And the third thing is that there are certain conveniences that just have to be designed in. As an additional security issue, people need places to store their possessions when they go into the laboratory. Sometimes these details are forgotten, and their absence truly affects the quality of life in the research environment.

Now a third aspect of the scientific enterprise, at least in life sciences, is that it is very interdisciplinary so communications between labs should be very easily accessible to the scientist. For instance, in a large research building, no matter how many elevators there are, waiting for the elevator is extremely frustrating when you want to travel to another floor to visit your colleague. On the other hand, the stairwells are always available and empty. Now it turns out that the stairwells in some buildings, and at the Rockefeller there are prominent examples, are dark and dingy and uninviting. They feel like territory that is off limits. I think this has been an overlooked part of the building. Stairs should be easy to walk up and down, a pleasant environment, so that people do not have to wait. Scientists are always pressed for time, so providing easy alternate access also has a lot to do with the health and happiness of the scientific pursuit.

In the laboratories themselves, in the life sciences, science is driven by experimentation. We are not armchair individuals. Today, a scientist cannot expect that he will read the literature and have an idea that someone else has not had simply because he is smarter than everyone else. There are a few individuals like that. I have met a couple. But that is not typical. This means that the way science progresses, and the way that one actually progresses within a field, is that one has information available that other people do not have. If I do an experiment that gives me a new piece of information that you do not have, then I may have an idea that is of value sooner than you do. So the laboratory itself, the actual bench space, is the heart of the laboratory and will continue to be in the life sciences always. And that means that the actual layout of the benches is extremely important.

The footprint of the building will dictate some aspects of how the laboratory itself is designed. For the life sciences, a ratio as close to 1 : 1 between lab space and support space is realistic in establishing the proportions of the floor plate. There are many procedures now being done in life sciences laboratories that are best done in isolated facilities or small rooms that might be commonly used by the investigators and should not be done on open benches in the labs. For example, my laboratory does a lot of work with radioactive isotopes. If you are doing an experiment with 50 millicuries, you do not want to do it with another investigator right next to you. Special procedure rooms must be extremely flexible, since needs change as you move through the scientific exercise. Places to handle animals and hazardous materials separate from the rest of the life of the laboratory are also important.

There are individuals within the laboratories who are bothered by experimentation with animals. It is not desirable to have some of the more graphic animal experimentation done in the laboratory itself. These experiments can offend even other scientists. Work such as this requires some security. So I think that it is critical to have extreme flexibility within the laboratories in the bench space, but also the support space has to be extremely flexible to accommodate the specific needs of different scientists.

Now one thing that is true is that electronic publishing and data handling are a growing part of biologic science. We no longer just present our data as photographs. Frequently, slides are digitized and the readout is printed out by computer. Good computer facilities, and in particular good imaging processing facilities in the life sciences, are going to be an integral part of every laboratory. So the dark room that is now critical and is designed into every lab may not exist in the laboratories of the future.

One of the things that I touched on earlier was the use of animals. In many universities, the care of animals is centralized. I think that is a good idea. However, due to the transportation of animals through the halls and people's objections to the use of animals, I think that each laboratory should have, in the life sciences, some facility for acute care and use of animals on the laboratory floors. This would avoid the need to constantly wheel experimental subjects throughout the university and will avoid exposure to people who are sensitive about this issue.

Both the hazardous materials and the animal care regulatory statutes will grow more difficult to satisfy. Designing in the sort of futuristic features to manage wastes automatically and to deal with the anticipated changes in the way we do science will be important.

I would like to conclude with some broader reflections on how the landscape of science is changing and what it may mean for facilities. Recently I have been interested in how the science I do might be utilized for the public. What this really means is trying to decide the venue whereby things that you do might be developed for biomedical purposes. Scientists in the life sciences are changing the way they look at how this might occur. In the past, it was typically the case that you might go to a large pharmaceutical firm, indicate that you have some useful research, and offer them the opportunity, or rather solicit their interest in developing it. There would be some interchange, you would get some kind of reward for that, and the project continues on in the large pharmaceutical house without your direct participation or control. I think that this will always be present within the research community. But it is being viewed now as less attractive than many other possibilities, such as, for example, starting your own company or starting a small biotech firm and retaining control over the research and the rewards. And there is a good reason for that.

Scientists, if they have worked on something for 15 years and brought it to the point of development, do not want to turn it over wholesale to someone else, even if they cannot do the research themselves in their own academic institution. We are confident of our abilities, and as professionals, we too have our egos.

We are trained for it. But there is now available, in many cases, the option of becoming associated with a small company where one can still direct the research into an applied direction. You can see in the media that there are many biotech startups. Many of them fail, but this is not going to go away.

Designing *small* research facilities to accommodate this fact of life now in science is something that is very important. I think all of the constraints on designing such a facility are not much different than designing a new research building in a university or a major pharmaceutical house. So, I think that one could, in a very specialized topic, create a company that had maybe 6 or 7 very focused laboratories, make a significant impact on a particular topic, and be successful.

Given this perception by the scientists at the universities who generate most of the fundamental research, I think there is going to be a lot of pressure in two directions. One is to have these kinds of small-scale mixed research and development facilities accessible to the universities themselves in the same area. In New York, these things could sprout up near the city so that the scientists involved can travel in between very easily. Second, I think that this will be important to the way universities view these ventures and may lead to them having a very active role in these small ventures themselves.

So the licensing of whatever we do may not be the most attractive option for the university. It may be that the interaction between the scientists at the university and these small satellite facilities becomes stronger and more serious than it had been in the past.

I will close by saying I think that the heart of the laboratory will not change in the life sciences in that we are experimentally driven. We will continue to do bench science. I cannot see that there is going to be another way to do it. Most scientists are driven by a love for the process of doing science. The experiment itself is part of our nature. It is not our object to become managers and manage other people doing the experiments, although that is almost an inevitable consequence of success.

The scientist's love of experimentation means that the core laboratory itself, the actual conduit of wet bench experiments, will probably not change. It will always be the central aspect of a laboratory. But the way the support space and flexibility are handled is going to be extremely important.

I think that the new building at Rockefeller goes a very long way in satisfying all these things. My experience has been that when people come through the university—job prospects and top-notch scientists—their positive reaction to the building pushes them a long way towards making a decision to come to Rockefeller. You should keep that in mind. It is extremely important that the laboratory space be attractive and first rate.

Physical Sciences Outlook

SAMUEL J. WILLIAMSON

Department of Physics and Center for Neural Science
New York University
2 Washington Place
New York, New York 10003

INTRODUCTION

"Flexibility" and "effective communication" are two major themes that will influence designs for the scientific workplace as we approach the next century. Traditional organizational boundaries of departments are tending to fragment, with individual faculty or research groups spinning off to form multidisciplinary alliances that focus on a common, broad topic. There is growing need for more effective communication between experts in disciplines who hardly talked with one another 20 years ago. No longer is science best served by segregating different disciplines in buildings separated by large stretches of green grass. Some researchers and administrators even take the point of view that many of the most exciting scientific developments will be forged at the interfaces between traditional disciplines.

Thus, there is an increasing need for architectural approaches that provide bridges between departments and between groups within larger interdisciplinary organizations. All of the features of architectural design that enhance communication across disciplines will also benefit cross-fertilization of ideas within any single discipline. In large part, the substance of this article comes from my own professional experience, first as a traditional physicist and more recently as a scientist who uses the instruments and certain conceptual frameworks of physics to carry out research on the functional organization of the human brain. Consequently, I will emphasize the viewpoint of the physical sciences, but most of this message is more general.

EVOLVING ORGANIZATION OF RESEARCH

The growing importance of interactions between disciplines is illustrated by a recent example: the emergence of cognitive neuroscience as a recognized specialty. FIGURE 1 depicts the intersection of developments in theoretical modeling, physical measurements, and quantitative analysis that unite aspects of psychology, physics, and mathematics for investigations of higher brain functions. This produced a new discipline known as *cognitive science*. Many researchers prefer this term over the more traditional one of cognitive psychol-

15

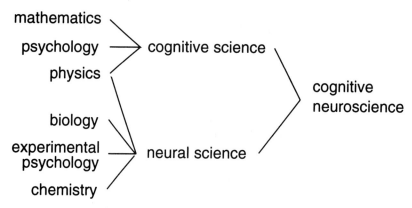

FIGURE 1. An example of the interactions between researchers in basic disciplines that lead to new disciplines.

ogy to emphasize their use of more sophisticated modeling and mathematical analysis. Similarly, the combination of biology, experimental psychology (physiology), and chemistry–together with dynamical concepts and instrumentation borrowed from disciplines such as physics–forms the basis for *neural science.* Its emphasis is on the understanding of the functions of single cells, of cell populations, and of the interactions between populations in different regions of the brain to explain development and sensory functions. The resulting overlap of cognitive science and neural science produces the hybrid discipline of *cognitive neuroscience.*

A similar evolution can be seen in the academic programs of major universities: more courses are team taught by faculty from diverse departments, even at the graduate level. This involvement has caused some colleagues to divert the main thrust of their research as they come to better appreciate fertile prospects for applying their specialties in new areas. There is every reason to expect this trend to continue, and even accelerate. It is becoming progressively more difficult to predict what a researcher will be doing 10, 20, or 30 years from now. The same can be said for the function of a science building.

Accompanying these changes in research and academic emphasis is an evolution in the way researchers communicate. Electronic mail–in particular– provides interactive communication at the press of a finger with individuals or groups at diverse locations. E-mail is becoming an essential component of the modern research enterprise, and those who avoid it are at a distinct disadvantage. Remarkably, even with such tools, researchers feel the need to speak personally with colleagues, eye to eye, just as in the business world. Creative ideas often come from the spontaneity of the give and take of discussions over a cup of coffee, or during a chance meeting in a hallway.

I am unable to recall a single instance when a meeting was planned to develop a great idea and succeeded in that task! Conceptual advances involving the participation of colleagues have come during unplanned, informal discussions. The design of science facilities should encourage these interactions.

PRIVATE AND PUBLIC SPACES

One way to think of space in a research building is to divide it into *private space* as expressed by offices and *public space* which is intended for individuals to meet each other. Private space is where a person can control access, so it is possible to mentally concentrate. The division into private and public spaces may not be always clear. For instance, at least one innovative design for a modern laboratory has public corridors pass through research laboratories in an attempt to enhance communications between passersby and workers. I would argue in this instance the choice is wrong. A typical researcher conducting experiments must fully concentrate and does not want such distractions. Labs should be private spaces, generally limited to the people who do research there.

On the other hand, scientists need to escape periodically from the pressures of concentrated research. These moments provide opportunity for a change of pace, and many researchers use the opportunity to meet with colleagues. ''Break spaces'' are public spaces, and they can be designed to enhance these interactions. Logical places are where people tend to congregate while attending to personal needs such as the mail room, department office, or coffee dispenser. A helpful design goal is to encourage researchers to linger and engage in discussions during these breaks. Obviously, such areas should be visually attractive, possibly featuring a different style of furnishing than the office or lab, to provide a refreshing experience.

FIGURE 2 shows an example of a research building erected in the mid-1960s that affords considerable flexibility and opportunity for personal interactions. Designed by the architectural and engineering firm of Albert C. Martin and Associates as the Science Center for the North American Aviation Corporation (now Rockwell International Corporation), the structure features a high degree of flexibility at low cost. Many design concepts were improvements on the features of the AT&T Bell Laboratories in Murray Hill, New Jersey, as many of the original staff came from that laboratory.

The external columns are structural elements of the building, with offices and laboratories on a single floor elevated above the natural terrain. This two-level design allows outsized or noisy equipment (vacuum pumps, for example) to be separately mounted on a column reaching up from the ground to nearly floor level of the lab, or suspended on a platform beneath the floorplate. Similarly, services such as gases are provided by simply running pipes beneath the floor and entering the laboratory by holes drilled through

FIGURE 2. Facade of the Science Center of the Rockwell International Corporation, showing external columns and the elevated floor for offices and laboratories. The open space below provides service facilities. (Courtesy of Rockwell Science Center.)

the floor. Service facilities such as loading dock and cafeteria are placed on the ground level.

COMMUNICATING SPACE

The Rockwell Science Center emphasizes two important concepts in design: *flexibility* in organization to respond to the ever-changing balance of research needs, and *enhancement of communication,* so that individuals readily meet each other. Flexibility is afforded by the interior construction: laboratory and office walls are of steel stud and wallboard, which permits easy renovation and affords a more soundproof wall than metal partitioning. Rear and side walls of the laboratories can also be removed if larger areas of contiguous space are needed.

Public spaces such as corridors and stairways are designed to enhance personal interactions. Wide stairways provide such a venue, especially because there is a comfortable bannister to lean against. Stairways are all the more effective for this purpose if corridors direct foot traffic toward them. FIGURE 3 illustrates the principle in a simple way. The arrangement of offices, labs, and corridors focuses on two stairways. Each was designed with unusual width to provide an open place to stop and talk, without getting in the way of colleagues passing by. Considerable traffic passes by the stair to reach the cafeteria and snack bar on the lower level–thus enhancing the prospect for interactions. In other types of buildings, communication can be facilitated at intersecting hallways by conveniently placed coffee nooks for break spaces.

Another effective aspect in this design is the placement of offices. Most of them run along the outer walls of the building, where they afford splendid views of the southern California countryside. The remaining offices encircle two open patios planted with attractive trees and shrubs. This pleasant environment is very much appreciated, and the dramatic contrast with interior features has been credited with encouraging new thoughts. Directly across the corridor from each experimentalist's office is the laboratory assigned to that person. This arrangement provides maximum convenience, since researchers frequency move from one space to the other.

Granted, there are few opportunities to design a "dream lab" like that of the Rockwell Science Center; nevertheless, useful lessons can be learned from the successful principles it exhibits. By contrast, we can consider a less successful example displayed by a vertically arranged structure. The complex for classrooms, offices, and laboratories shown schematically in FIGURE 4 actually consists of two separate buildings of 11 floors, a new one at the left and a renovated, old one at the right. Two small elevators at the juncture of the buildings provide the principal means for vertical movement. An adjacent stairway behind the elevator is often used for going between one or two floors; but it is comparatively narrow and does not provide an attractive

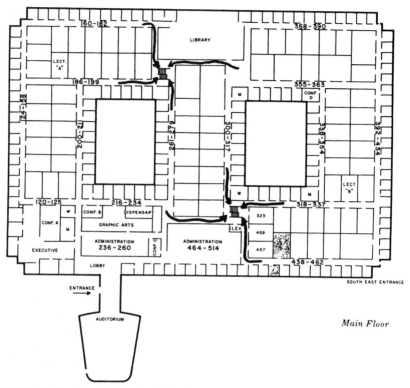

FIGURE 3. Plan for the interior of the Rockwell Science Center with arrows depicting converging routes to the two sets of generous stairways that lead to the lower level.

environment. These buildings are reasonably secure; nevertheless, students feel uncomfortable being alone in the stairwell during off hours.

The plan at the bottom of FIGURE 4 shows another shortcoming: the corridor in each building is rather short, so the number of colleagues one encounters late at night is small. Moreover, the corridors in the two buildings are offset, so that students and staff in each building see little evidence of the others when working at night. This imposes a feeling of isolation and insecurity. With longer corridors, and consequently a greater chance of seeing colleagues, there would be a more supportive feeling of being in a community. Group pressure would also be more effective in encouraging students to work late. Labs should be designed to encourage late-night use. This is often when the best experimental work is done! Not only are there fewer interruptions for committee meetings and telephone calls, but it is likely that various forms of environmental noise will be lower (more on this topic later).

Tall, thin buildings may look impressive from the outside, but interactions are greatly impeded when researchers are separated by even a single set of

Labs			Labs/Offices
Offices			Offices

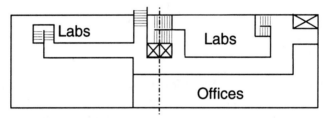

FIGURE 4. Schematic of the elevation and plan for a complex of two 11-story buildings with comparatively poor communication between floors. At the center are two small passenger elevators complemented by a narrow back stairway. A freight elevator in the corner is too slow to be effective for passengers, and stairways at each end of the building are so far from the center of action that they are rarely used.

stairs. This is especially true if stairways are not attractive. However, if the research building must be tall because of limited land space, one could imagine a wonderful solution to the problem of the building depicted in FIGURE 4. Instead of hiding the center stairway, make it a focal point by opening it to view. Wrap the stairway around the elevators, and install glass walls between elevators and stairs, in the old European apartment-house style. This would permit wider and more attractive stairs and would open the space to display the movement of the elevator. If hotels draw tourists by such a display, would it not provide a similar sense of fun and dynamism to professionals and staff in the building? More importantly, the loss in floor area and additional cost would be counterbalanced by encouraging more effective communication between floors.

Another deficiency can be seen in the floor plan of FIGURE 4: There are no break-out spaces. The corridors are lined by offices and labs, and it is necessary to go to the fourth or sixth floor to find public areas. Many–if not most–researchers in universities bring brown bag lunches and would be interested in gathering at an attractive table near the labs. At other times, such an area can also serve as a break-out space for reading or discussions.

LABORATORY SPACE

Traditionally, the biologist's office has been an integral part of the lab; whereas the physical scientist's is separate. This tradition may have arisen because a typical physical laboratory is not a pleasant environment. Aside from the visual impression of mechanical devices, cable trays, electronic instrument racks, and the like, there may be obnoxious features such as the noise and smell of vacuum pumps, optical experiments that require turning off the lights periodically, sensitive measurements prohibiting any movement at critical moments, and so forth. Also, experimental work in the physical sciences is often a group effort, so there is little privacy in a lab. For reasons such as this, personnel usually have separate office space. There it is helpful to establish a contrasting environment from that of the lab–carpets, windows, and a refreshing, comfortable atmosphere are most welcome.

It is worth emphasizing that laboratory space for physics and engineering research has a markedly different design from that of the biomedical sciences. The latter facilities usually feature modular work spaces, with a lab bench, desk, and support facilities. Often the layout follows a standard design that is replicated for each faculty member and includes the office. For such labs of the biological sciences, it is highly desirable to have windows in the laboratory to provide an attractive ambiance.

The situation is quite different in the physical sciences: Windows are generally not wanted in the lab! This feature is emphasized in the plan of the Rockwell Science Center (FIG. 3) where none of the labs have windows! Walls of a lab are valuable as a place for cabinets for storage of instruments and parts, and they are frequently used to support the experimental apparatus. There is no canonical set of furniture or equipment that is appropriate for a lab in the physical sciences. Every lab is different, and is likely to be modified for the purpose of the specific research. For these reasons, wall mountings are most useful if shelves and wall cabinets can be arranged on vertical runners at easily adjustable heights. Wall cabinets with glass fronts are often preferred because of the relative ease in finding a desired item.

It is usually best in a physical science lab to have ceilings and light fixtures at maximum height, with air ducts and fire sprinkler systems also kept as close to the ceiling as possible. This maximizes the usable height for accommodating an experimental setup. An example of the need for height is illustrated in FIGURE 5, which shows the author's laboratory for conducting experiments at extremely low temperatures, installed on the ninth floor of

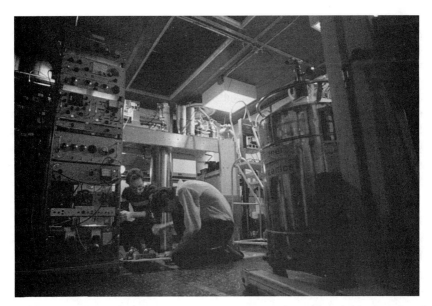

FIGURE 5. Facility for producing very low temperatures for studies of the properties of unusual materials. The entire setup is enclosed within a radiofrequency shielded room. A massive wood bridge mounted on vibration-isolated piers supports a cryogenic refrigerator that achieves a temperature of 3 mK on the ninth floor of a building in Manhattan, directly over a subway line. Above the bridge is a cupola that provides additional shielded space for lowering parts of the apparatus into the low-temperature environment. Below the bridge, a large hole cut through the floor permits the cryogenic enclosure to be lowered to gain access to the interior when required to make adjustments.

the Meyer Hall of Physics at New York University. This sensitive experiment had to be isolated from radiofrequency interference, so a large shielded enclosure of about 6 m × 9 m floor area was installed to accommodate the cryogenic system. This room barely squeezed between the floor and the ceiling beams. Ceiling ventilation ducts running between the beams were removed to permit the installation of a cupola just above the main part of the apparatus.

To minimize vibration, the cryogenic apparatus was suspended from a wooden bridge supported by shock-mounted vertical columns at the ends. A hole was cut in the floor, so that the vacuum-insulated dewar surrounding the apparatus could be lowered to gain access to the interior. The outline of 1 m × 2.5 m was sufficiently large to accommodate the researcher when the apparatus needed to be adjusted. Unluckily, complications arose when the rectangular hole was cut in the floor, for no plans had been made during building construction to define the electrical wiring routes within the concrete floor to feed the ceiling lights in the room below (a lesson there!). But some were found when the workman's diamond saw cut through them. This produced quite a display of fireworks, since the construction crew overlooked the fact that cutting power to my lab did not cut power to the overhead lights in the room below.

Luckily, I was on good terms with my faculty colleague of the lab below, and a cinder block tower was installed from his floor to the bottom of my slab, to provide walls around the hole for support and soundproofing. A year later, holes were drilled near the bottom of the tower at my colleague's level to permit a laser beam generated in his lab to pass into the tower, so the beam could be reflected into the low-temperature environment as part of a collaborative research study.

In general, I am convinced that architects of physical science and engineering buildings should take seriously the adage: "Walls are to be moved and floors drilled." Laboratory design for the physical sciences should emphasize *flexibility.* Not only will the type of experiment that an individual does be likely to change once or twice in her or his professional life, but perhaps just as likely one researcher will be replaced by another who will bring in a whole new set of equipment.

COMPUTER NETWORKS

It is abundantly clear that computers will continue to play increasingly more important roles in scientific research. Already, many experiments are run by computers, either in a scheduled mode or in more flexible mode where the computer's control is adjusted to changing conditions of the experiment. The researcher, whether in the laboratory or office, wants to observe what is happening. This can be done with modern research instruments that are connected to the local area network. The full exploitation of this capability will require local communications links that are considerably more extensive than commonly exist.

A central issue in the design of electronic communication within a building is how to set up the appropriate links. At present, most networks are configured to serve an existing administrative structure. For instance, the chemistry department may have a hard-wired network that threads through the chemistry building; the biology department has its own network, and so forth. Each host computer generally has some software that was installed specifically for the support of members of the department. The traditional method for serving labs and offices is to install cable runs that extend from the host computer. What happens when labs and offices are not clustered according to departments? Suppose that a few members of the chemistry and biology departments are located closer to the center for neural science? For the convenience and economy of using the existing wiring, will they be required to use the neural science computer as their host? This would be the case unless a central computer facility is arranged with network communications between the various local area networks. The system can sort out communications packets on the network that embraces both chemistry and neural science and directs them to the appropriate host.

An alternative technology for the future is the packet radio system, whereby each computer has a small low-power radio that broadcasts over short distances to a central host computer also served by a radio. This provides the advantage of needing no cable connection; instead recognition signals are transmitted between computer and host so that individual packets of information are received by the proper host. In such an arrangement, a computer can be easily moved from one location to another, so long as it remains within range of the host. A possible disadvantage of this arrangement is the increase in electromagnetic radiation within the environment.

LIBRARIES

Libraries are an essential component of the research enterprise, and their role is also undergoing dramatic changes. While most of the services continue to be of the traditional kinds, researchers see the onset of a revolution in how scientific literature will be handled. Several professional societies are experimenting with computer publication, whereby the contents of an issue of a journal are provided on a computer file. With modern high-resolution graphics workstations, the text, figures, and photographs can be viewed to advantage in the individual researcher's office. If a reprint is wanted, it can be printed on the spot.

No doubt that a well-equipped research library with archival resources is essential for any first-rate research laboratory. So, too, are the professional librarians who provide an invaluable service in cataloging and informing researchers about resource materials. But we can expect that the mix of services will evolve dramatically. Remote access to optical disks now provides rapid access to citations and reference information from the researcher's desktop computer. With increasing use of mass storage on disk, allowing remote computer access to obtain the original information, there will be less walking and more sitting when perusing the contents of a library. Direct access should be available from the lab as well as office, for there are often periods of inactivity during an experiment when a researcher could make use of the time for such purposes. In this sense, the library will become a more accessible and immediate partner in scientific pursuits.

THE PHYSICAL ENVIRONMENT

Looking toward the future, we can anticipate that succeeding generations of laboratory instruments will provide ever greater sensitivity in characterizing physical properties. This enhancement may profoundly influence the environmental requirements for a laboratory building. For instance, the development of the scanning tunneling microscope (STM) provides an instrument that reveals the arrangement of individual atoms attached to the surface of a solid such as graphite or gold. Recently, it has even been possible to show the shape of a single molecule! Successful research of this sort requires good control of vibration–from air circulation systems, wind forces on the building, automobile traffic, subways, and the like. Some vibration isolation can be achieved with specialized air-suspension tables; however, a quiet building is also important for minimizing low-frequency components of vibration.

Similarly, the use of magnetic imaging devices such as the electron microscope imposes demands on the choice of site and selection of equipment. Typically, the dominant source of low-frequency electric and magnetic fields is the power system of a building. Choosing power transformers with inadequate yokes to confine the accompanying magnetic field can wreak havoc with sensitive devices, and has been known to influence more prosaic equipment like computer monitors nearby! Electrified mass-transportation systems similarly can produce magnetic fields at distances of 50 meters that cause serious deterioration in the performance of electron microscopes. These and other environmental factors merit increasing concern when planning scientific facilities.

EXAMPLE OF AN INTERDISCIPLINARY DEVELOPMENT

My own research on superconductivity and low-temperature physics led me about 20 years ago to wonder how the ultrasensitive devices we used in our experiments might have other applications. One such instrument–called a "SQUID" for superconducting quantum interference device–was the most sensitive instrument for measuring magnetic fields. Since the buildings of the departments of psychology and physics are contiguous (indeed, psychology was on the other side of my laboratory wall), it was natural to think about using the SQUID to locate neural activity in the human brain. Lloyd Kaufman (Professor of Psychology) thought likewise, so he and I formed a collaboration. It was lucky that a hole was found in the wall, high up near the ceiling so it was not easily seen. This let us pass a communication cable from the SQUID sensor in the physics building to the psychology building, where it was connected to a computer that could analyze the data. Later, when our collaboration strengthened, we replaced the hole by an official doorway installed in the wall, with stairs on one side because the floor levels of the different buildings were not commensurate. This allowed us to run back and forth directly, instead of making a major detour via the stairs that were provided in the original building plan.

Subsequently, when we acquired sufficient financial support, we also installed a commercial prefabricated magnetically shielded room for the SQUID and subject being studied. It has floor dimensions of 3 m × 4 m and height of 2.8 m. With overhead air ducts removed, it was still a tight fit into a standard lab room, just squeezing under the fire sprinkler pipe by 1 cm. It was also tight for weight, since its total of 8 tons was right at the weight limit for floor loading! Did the architect for this building ever imagine we would be putting such an object into this room? As the number of researchers in our group increased, we were allocated a few more adjacent laboratory rooms where computers were installed to analyze the ever-increasing load of data. To encourage interactions among our lab personnel, a large doorway was opened in the cinder-block wall that separated two of the rooms.

SUMMARY

In short, this personal experience emphasizes that no one can predict with any certainty what will be demanded of lab space in the future. Therefore, it is important to maintain a strong emphasis on *flexibility*. In the physical sciences, it is most helpful to design labs with generous space, especially in ceiling height. Nice-looking false-ceiling panels are not wanted! On the other hand, esthetic features are all the more important in break spaces such as corridors, stairways, lobbies, etc. The lab environment should be kept simple and designed for ease in making changes. Flexibility can be provided by free-standing cinder-block walls (better for sound insulation than common metal walls), with vertical runners that allow adjustment of fixtures such as shelves and cabinets. It is well to keep in mind that lab walls are meant to be moved and floors drilled.

Capital Investment Decision Making and Laboratory Renovations

STEPHEN M. COHEN

Office of the Associate Dean for Finance and Administration
Yale University School of Medicine
1-209 Sterling Hall of Medicine
333 Cedar Street
New Haven, Connecticut 06510

I will be speaking from the perspective of an institutional decision maker, in particular, from the institutional perspective of privately capitalized, but federally funded, research intensive medical schools in urban environments, which is a fairly accurate characterization of many leading biomedical research institutions including Harvard, Hopkins, Pennsylvania, Cornell, New York University, Columbia, Washington University, and so on.

I think, in the future, these private research intensive medical schools will be quite constrained with regard to the capital investment resources available to them. This is because the primary purchaser of the scientific knowledge they develop is the federal government, which exercises its leverage to write reimbursement rules that allow these institutions to earn only a partial return *of* their capital investment, never a return *on* the capital invested. Given, then, the limited capacity to retain from operating revenues the capital sums needed to invest in laboratory facilities, where will the funds come from to finance new laboratory renovation and construction projects? And how will the capital sums that are available be used?

It is true that a school can build a new laboratory building more cheaply, on a per-unit basis, than it can renovate its already existing laboratories. The problem is that new building decisions have to be made $40 million at a time, whereas a well-ordered, well-coordinated series of renovations could allow for the release of capital $3, $4, $5 million at a time. For a variety of reasons, but most importantly economic ones, private, urban, research intensive medical schools will continue to be in the renovation business, primarily because the management of the capital flows is much more flexible in terms of the amount of money that is committed to any one particular initiative. Given the need to make these types of investments, what role can financial analysis play in deciding which projects get done?

One of the things that is most perplexing about capital planning and analysis at universities and medical schools is how generally primitive the tools are for evaluating financial returns on physical capital. We go to great lengths at Yale to measure, estimate, and project the risk and return on our financial capital. We have very sophisticated ways of looking at our portfolio of financial capital, distributing it among different internal and external decision makers, and incorporating that capital income in our program plans. All this is done for what we would consider to be passive income.

The replacement value of our physical endowment is one and a half times that of our financial endowment, and we use that (physical) capital investment to generate active returns. That is to say, we have investigators like Dr. Heintz or Dr. Williamson who are able to generate significant research revenues from sponsored projects. Unfortunately, we have not yet developed the tools necessary to measure the rates of financial return that would enable us to make intelligent decisions about investments in physical capital. Although some progress has been made in this regard, we are still a long way from effectively utilizing financial decision-making rules for investments in capital projects.

Because of the constraints on available capital, and as Dr. Williamson said, because the advances in science render our laboratories suboptimal in 10-15 years, medical schools must have more sophisticated capabilities in financially planning and carrying out a series of renovations. There is already a very large stock of existing laboratory space in this country's universities and research institutes, and unless the real rate of growth in the scientific marketplace exceeds the real rate of growth in the overall gross domestic product, this existing space should carry us well into the next century. As an institutional purchaser, therefore, I am looking for ways to evaluate the scale of a particular renovation project so that I am recycling my institution's stock of space in the most cost-effective but scientifically flexible manner.

Complementing the need to develop better ways of financially analyzing and planning renovation projects is the need to price our science better than we have in the past. I think we must become more skilled at determining what is the real capital-consumption cost attributable to a particular scientific project or series of projects, and then negotiate better with the sponsors of that science for funding of capital maintenance.

I appreciate the opportunity to come here today and am looking forward to enhancing my ability to make appropriate decisions about investments in laboratory facilities. Not only is biomedical science a capital intensive enterprise, but that capital is very expensive to maintain. If we are able to minimize that cost through effective planning and maintenance, and if we can continue to develop young scientists so that they become as productive as Drs. Heintz and Williamson, then I am convinced that society will provide our institutions with the financial resources necessary to invest in its scientific laboratories.

The challenge to institutional managers and policy makers is to balance both society's and the institution's return on invested capital with the return on invested science.

Future Trends in Science, Technology, Politics, Social Behavior, and Economics that May Influence Research Facility Design—Causes and Trends

Managerial Outlook—Corporate Side

LEON L. LEWIS

Hoffmann-La Roche Inc.
Nutley, New Jersey 07110

We live in a world driven by accelerating change, orchestrated through science, technology, politics, social behavior, and economics. Merely keeping pace with the normal pressures for change requires an increasingly more accurate and insightful vision of the future. That vision must constantly be cast out further in time in order to avoid a collision with the present. The pace and cost of change leave little room for error. Accurately projecting future trends and needs demands a comprehensive understanding of the present and its relationship to the past.

Few research drivers for change move forward in isolation. Their direction and velocity are constantly modified by other scientific and technological discoveries, social and economic changes, local and world conditions, human behavior and evolution. Research facilities are meant to complement the research effort. In a millennium of fast-flowing discovery and technology, how can motionless, structured resources possibly avoid impeding the progress of science, unless there is a clear understanding of scientific goals, objectives, directions, and pace? Thus, managing today's research resources requires an enlightened vision of the future.

Medically oriented science and technology are primarily centered within academic institutions, private research organizations, industrial corporations, and governmental resources. The following discussion highlights several driving forces and trends influencing research facility design within the research-based pharmaceutical industry. Pharmaceuticals offer numerous benefits in the treatment of major diseases. The reduction in overall health care costs resulting from reduced hospital and surgical expenses may be as important as the therapeutic advantages of effective drug treatment. Unfortunately, the cost of pharmaceutical development is high. It takes 10 or more years to bring a new drug to market at a cost often exceeding $300,000,000. In the process, over one-half of the patent protection life of the new drug will have been consumed in the development process. The dropout rate among new drug candidates is high. Only one in approximately 5000 results in marketed new product.

The majority of new drugs are discovered, developed, and marketed within the research-based pharmaceutical industry. In an increasingly global, highly competitive, risk-prone environment, individual corporations must create well-managed, flexible, and dynamic research organizations that can rapidly respond to new therapeutic opportunities throughout the world. There appears to be a trend toward larger international pharmaceutical corporations, achieved through acquisitions, partnerships, and licensing arrangements. With a focus on total quality management (TQM) and cutting edge science, the major corporations seek to speed the discovery process, reduce development time, and accelerate the time to market.

At the same time, advances in science are opening enormous new avenues of therapeutic opportunity through biotechnology. Small, innovative companies are using the cutting-edge tools of molecular genetics and biology to create new treatment applications and advanced understanding of the disease process. With increasing frequency, major pharmaceutical corporations are providing financial and scientific support to biotechnology companies, while respecting the need for uninhibited scientific exploration.

Responding to the challenge to develop dynamic research programs that can rapidly seize new therapeutic opportunities, a significant number of pharmaceutical corporations have reorganized their research groups into therapeutic categories. Gone are the traditional scientific departments of pharmacology, biochemistry, molecular genetics, drug metabolism, etc. In their place are interdisciplinary groups of scientists focusing on opportunities in oncology, cardiovascular problems, central nervous system disorders, inflammation, pulmonary disease, and others. The management structure stresses horizontal and vertical communication within and outside of research (sales, marketing, project management, research, and corporate management); all participants working to optimize scientific breakthroughs leading to new products. With its focus on productive and timely interaction, the system imposes new demands on research facility design to stimulate open communication and rapid, cost-effective adaptation to shifting research priorities.

With this overview, it is possible to explore a number of additional trends that appear to have the potential to significantly alter pharmaceutical research. Ultimately, the design and pace of development and redevelopment of research facilities may be impacted by these factors. In terms of facility construction and design, the following issues are potential decisional drivers:

- Changes in the medical health care delivery system.

- Industry investment in research and development.

- Industry support for academic research.

- Outsourcing of research and services.

It seems safe to predict there will be changes in the health care delivery system within the United States. The form, timing, and magnitude of change remain much debated issues. The intensity of the discussions has already begun to reshape the pharmaceutical industry. Prominent changes include:

1. Voluntary control of the prices of marketed pharmaceuticals.
2. Increased focus on low-cost generics.
3. Increased availability of over-the-counter versions of prescription pharmaceuticals.
4. Proposals related to the management of health care affecting:
   - how drugs are marketed and sold.
   - how drugs are selected.
5. Proposals to alter new drug patent protection regulations.

All of these issues directly or indirectly affect profitability. The impact is already being felt as corporations struggle to hold profit margins through reductions in operating expense and intensified global marketing. Workforce reductions are commonplace. For the first time in many years, these reductions are also occurring in the research and development sector. This is especially significant because the pharmaceutical industry is among the largest investors in research and development, as a percentage of gross sales. The current level of 12 to 15% far exceeds other research-based industries investing 5 to 6% per year.

If "form" really does follow "function," one would expect to begin to see an evolution in research facility design compatible with the dynamic changes occurring in the pharmaceutical research sector. Quite possibly the observed slowdown in the construction of new research facilities is reflective of the magnitude of change anticipated. Aside from the pace of new construction and redevelopment, a number of design considerations appear to match the evolving research management trends and scientific advancements. These include:

- Increased laboratory flexibility without significant cost penalty.

- Enhanced building efficiency in terms of:
  - net to gross ratios.

- energy costs.
- life cycle costs for maintenance.

- Lower occupancy costs per square foot.
    - higher occupancy densities outside the laboratory.
    - smaller offices.
    - reduced churn costs.
    - flexible furniture systems.

- Centralized support services.

- Functional integration of research disciplines into therapeutic opportunities.

- Natural integration.
    - ghost corridors.
    - open work stations.

- Immediate access to small group conference rooms within the laboratory complex.

- Enhanced outsourcing of service activities.

- Enhanced security during and after normal working hours.

In the past, public access to laboratory facilities was minimal. As the need to communicate the benefits of pharmaceutical research becomes more pressing, the desire to provide direct public contact with research activities may result in design modifications. Public meeting spaces, laboratory tours, and research displays are likely to become common in order to enhance:

- Public awareness of the benefits of pharmaceutical research.

- Public exposure to the laboratory environment and its scientists.

- Education of students to the career opportunities in science.

The design of research facilities is further influenced by the personal needs of scientists. Competition among pharmaceutical corporations for promising young scientists is intense. Recognition of the changing cultural and environmental needs of its employees has resulted in greater attention to:

- Libraries and reference resources.

- Seminar facilities.

- Fitness and wellness resources.

- Interior and exterior landscaping.
- Natural light.
- Furniture.
- Softer laboratory settings.
- Interaction space.
- Historic displays.
- Artwork and sculpture.
- Convenient parking.
- Day-care facilities.

As pharmaceutical research enters a period of extraordinary advancement in the treatment and diagnosis of human and animal diseases, the tools and resources of biological exploration must undergo equally impressive modification and evolution. We have identified some of the issues and factors that have stimulated new approaches to research facility management and design. Above all else, these directions must continue to complement our critical new research goals and objectives.

The View from Mars

DENNIS FLANAGAN

12 Gay Street
New York, New York 10014

I chose the title "The View from Mars" to emphasize the fact that I am not a scientist or an architect, but no kind of expert at all. I am, however, a professional spectator and have been for a long time. Listening to the speakers before me I have the sensation that the entire meeting is being held for my benefit, since I have so much to learn about the subject.

You will remember that when Martians began to arrive here after the Second World War, we were all surprised that they were so small. Their average height proved to be about two feet. One day a few years ago one of their tiny spacecraft came in for a landing on Third Avenue. Because of the traffic it had to stop short, and it blew a tire. The crew was quite concerned because they had already used their spare. Just then one of them looked up and saw a delicatessen window full of bagels. "Tires!" he shouted, and rushed into the delicatessen. "Give me one of those tires, quick." The counterman said: "Buddy, those aren't tires. They're bagels. They're good to eat. Here, try one." The Martian took the big bagel in his little hand and bit into it. "Say, that *is* good. I bet it would go good with lox."

The point of my story is that if people from Mars do not know everything, they do know a few things. In order to prepare for this talk I engaged two scientists as consultants. I did not pay them anything; they are my son, a molecular biologist at Harvard, and his wife, a physiologist at Tufts. Their strong feelings about the design of scientific laboratories closely parallel what Dr. Heintz has just been saying, so I should not bore you by repeating them. They did make a couple of other points. My son tells me that in the several laboratories where he has lived, he has always been frustrated by the lack of a private space for computer work. Although such work calls for concentration and quiet, the computer is usually out in the open on a laboratory bench. My daughter-in-law tells me that her laboratory is plagued by RF interference, which plays hob with their electronic instruments. This is a reminder that in the design of scientific laboratories the external environment is an important factor.

At this point, I think I may be able to make a small contribution to the discussion out of my own experience as both a worker and a boss in the publishing business. A curious phenomenon in journalism is the work space they call a bullpen. You may remember that in movies like *All the President's Men* and *Absence of Malice*, the journalists work in a huge open space flanked by a few glass-enclosed offices for the top editors. The rest of the people are lined up like clerks in an insurance company, although it is true that they walk in and out and put their feet up on the desk. When I first had to work in such a space, I found it quite disconcerting. I could not call my girlfriend without thinking I might be overheard, and when I sat down to write something, I was distracted by all the things going on around me. I finally adjusted, but you wonder if this is really necessary. I do not think it is. It is a reflection, which goes back a long way, of how the people who run the business feel about those queer ducks who actually put out the paper. You can save money by putting a lot of people in one large space.

That one large space does have some advantages. You have to be careful not to interrupt colleagues who are pounding away at their keyboard, but on the other hand you can see them sitting there, and if you need to consult with them about something or other, you can conveniently do so. Dr. Heintz and others here have been referring to coffee space, tea space, seminar space– I gather the official architects' term is breakout space. I think it is being recognized that every worker needs *both* private space, however modest, and public space. You may have seen a story in *The New York Times* last week about how Apple Computer had come to this conclusion. It is not only the gung-ho high-tech companies who need such arrangements.

There is a kind of corollary to a worker's needing both private and public space. The boss's space needs to be more public than it often is. A boss should be a person who is accessible to the worker, not some kind of pope who occasionally emerges to give orders. This is particularly true in the kind of work I have done for most of my life: editing a magazine. If you are to get the show on the road, your door simply *must* be open. No editor can predict *all* the problems that his colleagues are going to encounter and that will need his approval or decision. You would not believe it, but I have known of editors who thought their job was to lock their door and think deep thoughts about the future. They did not last long. Somebody outside the door was always moaning "Who's going to O. K. this layout?" So to the extent that architecture can have an influence on the problem, I think that laboratory directors and other bosses should always be in a location where people can get at them.

Now I have a little entertainment for you that I hope will not be entirely irrelevant. Originally I was asked if I would give a talk on how science might be evolving in the future, and what influence that might conceivably have on the architecture of laboratories. I would not be so rash, particularly because I have always adhered to the view that the definition of a discovery is something we did not know before. The important discoveries by definition cannot be predicted, and when they are made, they always make monkeys out of futurologists.

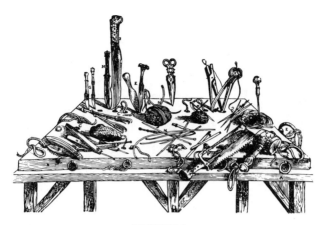

FIGURE 1

Still, it is easy to make out three areas where scientists will be concentrating their efforts in the coming decades. One is in physics, where leading theorists are striving, with the help of experimentalists, to devise a single mathematical theory that embraces all the basic phenomena of matter and energy. The other two are in biology. Biologists–and the rest of us too– would like to know how the brain works and how a single cell, the fertilized egg cell, develops into an entire organism. Therefore the stakes for creating good working environments in biological laboratories are high.

Okay. In order to look forward, it is always helpful to look backward (FIG. 1). What you see here is a laboratory bench of the 16th century, the year 1543 to be exact. It is the bench of Andreas Vesalius, a Belgian physician who was certainly one of the greatest scientific discoverers of all time. He has been called the discoverer of the human body, and some historians regard him as the founder of modern biology. I think you can figure out what some of the things on the bench are: knives, saws, clamps and the like. Vesalius used them to cut up the human body and figure out how it was made. He was not the first to dissect the body. In fact, medical students of the 16th century observed dissections all the time–from their seats in the lecture hall. I mean the students did not do the dissections themselves. That was done by barber surgeons, ignorant men who hacked up the body as though they were working in a butcher shop. Even worse, what the students read about anatomy was based on the writings of the Greek physician Galen. He too was a great man, but he had worked more than 1000 years earlier in the second century A.D.

What Vesalius did was to do the dissections himself, with the eye of a physician who could understand what he was doing. One of the first things he discovered was that he could not find some of the anatomical structures

FIGURE 2

described by Galen. The mystery was solved when Vesalius happened to dissect an ape. There he found the missing structures. It suddenly dawned on him that Galen's anatomy was based not on the human body but on the bodies of apes.

We hear a lot these days about the unfortunate separation of art and science. As anyone knows who has a nodding acquaintance with Renaissance artists, this was not always the case. The artists were *au courant* with science and mathematics and much stimulated by them. One artist was so excited by the work of Vesalius that his pictures became an integral part of Vesalius's work. We are not quite sure about his identity, but the best guess appears to be that he was Jan van Calcar, a Flemish artist who worked in the workshop of the mighty Titian. Titian, of course, was Venetian, and Vesalius lectured at the medical school in the neighboring city of Padua.

At first Vesalius could not go against the ingrained custom of the dissections being done by barber surgeons, so he had to get the necessary cadavers on the sly. One source was condemned criminals whose bodies were left hanging on the gallows as an object lesson. That may partly explain why the bodies are strung up the way they are in the pictures I am about to show you.

I think I will let you look at my next slide in silence for a few moments (FIG. 2). It is obvious that the artist was doing a good deal more than simply

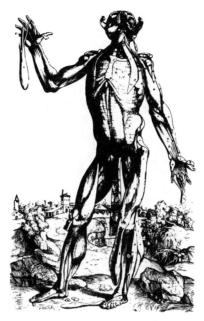

FIGURE 3

illustrating the dissected body. For him the experience was highly dramatic—both scientifically and artistically. You may have noticed some of the details. The diaphragm has been removed and nailed to the wall. The muscles of the forearm have been dissected out and allowed to hang down.

This is only one of more than 100 illustrations the artist made for Vesalius's great book *De humani corporis fabrica*—the structure of the human body. He traced the dissection of the body from beginning to end (FIGS. 3, 4, and 5). The technique was woodcut, a most demanding one. An interesting sidelight is that the wood blocks were still in existence 400 years later. Then they were destroyed in a Second World War bombing of Munich.

Now I am going to run those last three slides backward. If you look closely, you'll see that the artist added a delightful embellishment. The landscape in the background continues from one figure to another. It is a landscape in the hills outside Padua.

Vesalius dissected not only the various parts of the body but also the circulatory system (FIG. 6). He did not perceive that the blood circulated, as William Harvey did 70 years later.

The text of Vesalius's book was quite undistinguished and even in those days was not much read. It was the marvelous pictures that did it all. Even today when you see a full-figure drawing of the human anatomy in a dictionary

FIGURE 4

FIGURE 5

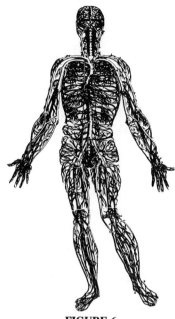

FIGURE 6

or an encyclopedia the chances are that it looks very much like one of them. Such drawings are based on scientific illustrations made 450 years ago, in the same year that Copernicus wrote that the earth goes around the sun. I would go so far as to say that this is the first true scientific art and the best. It has never been surpassed.

The point I am trying to make is that when you think about the excitement reflected in this marriage of science and art, you have to regret that it no longer exists. Furthermore, it implies the profound role of imagination in scientific creation. I haven't the faintest idea of how such a thing could be implemented, but somewhere in the design of working spaces for scientists, room has to be left for the imagination. Thank you.

Roundtable Discussion

The Outlook of the Scientific Community —Future Trends

SUMMARY

The roundtable discussion probed more deeply into the agenda of discernible scientific, social, and economic trends and concerns that will guide the design of future research and development facilities. Participating in the discussion were all of the morning speakers (Cohen, Flannagan, Heintz, Lewis, Williamson) along with architect Leevi Kiil, construction manager Anthony Winson, and Stanley Stark as moderator.

Many issues received attention: more facilities for fewer dollars, adaptability, the changing nature of organizational settings, measurements of investment utility. Diversity led to both illumination and in some cases impasses, thus demonstrating that everything has a cost.

There was general agreement that, over time, there is a need to get more for less—greater return on investment, either societally or economically. It is a function of both competitiveness and limited resources. Predictably, scientists and managers offered different perspectives, all of which contributed to a broader picture of an increasingly complex laboratory environment. It was acknowledged that the way science will be conducted is changing: that scientists will not just operate within labs under the central control of a university or large corporation. The change in the ways in which scientific research is being organized will determine changes in facility design. Furthermore, the trend toward industrial and university science becoming more corporate in its organization might well change decisions about what actually gets built.

REMAINING BARRIERS

There was agreement that we need to think about what elements of the R&D process we want to cause to interact—not just within disciplines, but between them. This interaction will be where the new science will be, where the new, interesting things are going to happen. The bringing together of different scientific disciplines will create a whole new way of looking at science. Removing barriers and encouraging such interdisciplinary interchange will be important to the conduct of science. Therefore, it is an important issue to plan into facilities.

The same is true in terms of the relationships between management and scientists. Mr. Kiil offered that it is precisely the sort of open, cross-disciplinary dialogue occurring at this conference that is necessary on a project basis as the key to address needs of user and management to meld individual viewpoints and seek the best design solutions. This view was reinforced by Dr. Lewis.

ORGANIZATIONAL SETTINGS

Dr. Lewis expressed concern that the mega pharmaceutical companies will consume all the talent.

Dr. Heintz differed. He does not see the mode of centralization of mega corporations affecting university science, although he does see the growing attraction for top investigators to form small companies. He questioned whether the large pharmaceutical firms are likely to be a favored setting for top-tier scientific talent.

WHAT ARE WE MISSING?

Dr. Williamson highlighted two issues affecting design that require our attention. Among specific changes being seen in organization and process, as we convert to electronic storage of data, decisions have to be made about what will be kept in paper and what on computer file, which will pose a design challenge for what has traditionally been the library. He was also the first to voice the need to give greater weight to the work conditions and housing of graduate students, who seem to be the lowest priority in academic research facility design.

Mr. Flannagan pointed out that a great many experimental sciences are not fundamentally lab based (e.g., social sciences, psychology, archeology). Yet, they too have needs that have not been directly addressed (office space, storage, data systems, observational spaces, team spaces, etc.). Mr. Stark articulated another trend, the increasing loading of offices with heat-generating equipment. Offices are resembling lab support spaces. Both their configurations and design criteria need to be reconsidered.

MEANING OF THE VALUE OF INVESTMENT

Mr. Cohen pointed out the major conundrum that much of the decision making in the academic environment is controlled by staff and executives who lack the vocabulary and intuitive understanding of the nature or the complexity of R&D building projects. He asked that architects and engineers provide new tools of measurement and new vocabularies for discussion (e.g., employ a measure that can quantify output benefits per unit of investment). Evaluating projects on the basis of dollars per square foot simply results in false comparisons.

Drs. Heintz and Williamson, each in his own way, questioned the usefulness of trying to value lab output in terms of capital investment. Scientists and managers did not arrive at a common vocabulary as a result of this discussion.

General Discussion

Questions from the floor focused on concerns about distribution of shrinking funding and the organization of scientific teams, both internally and outside the research institute. There was discussion of how to bring together the right disciplines to get beyond basic discovery and facilitate its development by making the most of opportunities to share resources, discovery, development, application, and marketing. One participant expressed the concern that such interaction is not an additive but a geometric process. The issue of whether the worthiness of a research effort can be judged in terms of life cycle costing was raised.

Mr. Cohen responded that increased interaction will be more critical than ever in order to recognize the domain of each party in making financial decisions. He suggested that while measurements such as input and output cost ratios are useful in overall capital planning and institutional development to insure the continued financial health of an institution, he and his colleagues at Yale do not use them to benchmark the productivity of individual laboratories.

Dr. Heintz pointed out another trend is the changing organization of science. As federal support for science is reduced, universities will want to be equity partners instead of just licensing whatever technology is produced there.

Dr. Lewis predicted that we will see great innovation in partnerships in the next 10 years and said if the process of discovery, development, application, and marketing is to be a continuum, we need to structure it in such a way that it can be fostered by the facility.

The Issues of Lab Design and the Current State of the Art

The Research Manager's Viewpoint

LEON L. LEWIS

Hoffmann-La Roche Inc.
Nutley, New Jersey 07110

One must be impressed by the enormous size and diversity of research resources available within the United States. The buildings and facilities have supported the extraordinary advancement of academic, federal, and industrial science and research since the 1940s. It is somewhat of a shock to realize that many of these key structures are now 20 to 60 years of age. While the exterior building "shells" are often surprisingly well maintained, the interior floor plates and infrastructures no longer support the evolving requirements of modern science and technology. Remodeling of offices or laboratories and infrastructural upgrades are frustrated by overall space compression and the absence of usable swing space. As the cost of science has grown and the funding base for research has flattened and shifted, deferral of routine facility maintenance has become commonplace. This pattern is seen not only in older structures, but is a self-defeating characteristic of many new research buildings erected within the past 10 years.

The efficiency and effectiveness of research facilities are significantly affected by the culture that defines how individual scientists perform and function within their research environment. In the past, traditions of departmental or disciplinary research led to rigid ownership and boundaries, resource duplication, and horse trading. Global goals and objectives were often blurred by the instinctive desire for group survival. Under such cultures, only the strong get stronger. On such playing fields, research space planning remained on the forest floor. The view was limited to a few trees. This type of woodpeckering resulted in brushfire management.

The world of research is changing. The new paradigm establishes an interactive research culture that is dynamic, interdisciplinary, global, communicative, and goal oriented. Within pharmaceutical research, it moves toward an open, mobile, innovative scientific community structured to seize new therapeutic opportunities that lead to breakthrough treatments and cures. Within the new research culture, strategic space planning is essential. Facilities and resources must complement the accelerated pace of achievement.

There are many successful planning tools and techniques for assessment of research resource needs. A frequently used starting point is the evaluation of existing facilities in terms of current research goals and objectives; corporate or institutional cultural norms; established site plan requirements; research and administrative personnel profiles; modern research space and infrastructural standards or requirements; and the type, form, and size of support services required. This process is often referred to as "decompression analysis."

The scope and definition of decompression studies can be as narrow or broad as necessary to fully characterize the research organization in terms of facilities and resources. The following types of questions can easily be explored:

1. Do we have the correct amount of research space to meet our current goals and objectives? If there is a deficiency, where does it exist?
   research labs
   support labs
   special labs
   offices and workstation
   conference rooms
   libraries
   interaction zones
   storage space
   others
2. Do we have necessary support resources in terms of size, capacity, and quality of service?
   research shops
   glasswash
   animal resources
   research supplies
   maintenance
   receipt and delivery
   safety and environmental management
   others
3. How do our laboratory and support areas compare to modern laboratory standards and requirements?
   electrical power (normal and conditioned)
   emergency power
   laboratory gas distribution, quality and source
   lighting
   ventilation
   hood design and capacity
   storage
   linear feet of bench per scientist

> net square feet per scientist
> others

4. Are research adjacency requirements satisfied in terms of interactive associations?

> departments, groups, teams, and labs
> within or between floors, buildings, or sites
> others

The establishment of laboratory design standards is essential to the decompression analysis process. Most research institutions develop such standards based on consultation with professional designers, programmers and engineers. Benchmarking other research organizations is frequently utilized. The key to successful employment of standards is to seek internal input and consensus at the scientific and managerial level. However, the standards should be as dynamic and flexible as the current, evolving research matrix. Constant communication is essential to successful use of strategic planning standards.

Limited examples of several laboratory space standards currently utilized within the research and development sector of a major pharmaceutical corporation are provided for discussion purposes. The guidelines have specific application only to that organization and should not be viewed as generally applicable to other research operations.

1. Research Laboratory Space

> nsf   = net square feet.
> RLME = research laboratory module equivalent.
> BIOLOGY LABS   252 nsf / RLME
> CHEMISTRY LABS   315 nsf / RLME
> The RLME is an essential tool for normalizing space data from different buildings, constructed at different times, utilizing various space standards.

2. Research Laboratory Occupancy Density

> BIOLOGY LABS   1.5 Scientists / RLME
> CHEMISTRY LABS   1.5 Scientists / RLME
> Adjustment Factor:
> Adjustment must be made to provide 1.0 Senior Scientists / 2 RLME

3. Research Laboratory Bench Space

> LF   = linear feet
> BIOLOGY LABS   22 LF bench / Scientist
> CHEMISTRY LABS   28 LF bench / Scientist

4. Laboratory Offices (outside of labs)

> 80 nsf / Senior Scientist

5. Laboratory Workstation (outside of labs)
   42 nsf / Scientist
6. Equipment Support Laboratories
   RLME = Research Lab Module Equivalent
   ESME = Equipment Support Module Equivalent
   BIOLOGY   1.0 ESME / 3.0 RLME
   CHEMISTRY   1.0 ESME / 3.0 RLME
7. Special Support Labs
   RLME = Research Lab Module Equivalent
   SSME = Special Support Module Equivalent
   BIOLOGY   1.0 SSME / 2.0 to 5.0 RLME
   CHEMISTRY   1.0 SSME / 2.0 to 5.0 RLME
8. Administrative Support
   Includes administrative offices, workstation, conference rooms, mail and copy resources, file areas, and archive spaces.
   Programmed at the rate of 10% of the net square feet of laboratory space.

With the decompression data in hand, it is now possible to forecast future growth and development using the same common standards. There are three basic elements to consider:

Normal growth resulting from advances in research technology
   Calculated at the rate of 2 to 3%/year of the net square feet of decompressed laboratory space.
   Growth resulting from additional scientific personnel
   No. new scientists × decompression standards
Growth or downsizing resulting from strategic considerations.
   Business plan
   Research plan
   Other considerations

The application of techniques similar to the ones described above offers a most useful tool in the strategic planning of research space requirements. As we move forward into a period of intense scientific discovery and application, the ability to anticipate resource needs well in advance of their activation is critical to success. At the same time, the growing changes in the way biomedical research is conducted are beginning to alter the priorities of laboratory design. While laws, regulations, and standards redefine the engineering elements of laboratory hoods, benches, and ventilation systems, the interdisciplinary research structure has begun to influence building orientation in terms of communication and resource sharing. Advances in research technology are driving changes in infrastructural requirements and the need for enhanced flexibility without significant cost penalty.

The challenge and the excitement lie in our ability to provide facilities and resources that complement the research effort. In so doing, we become a part of its beauty and passion.

The Generic Planning Process

ROBERT H. McGHEE

Research Facility Planning
Howard Hughes Medical Institute
2401 Wroxton Road
Houston, Texas 77005

The Howard Hughes Medical Institute sold the Hughes Aircraft Company to General Motors in 1985. That created the opportunity to expand the research program and corresponding facility program. The Institute started a building program of 13 new buildings, mostly for scientists who had not yet been identified or recruited. The general area of their work was known and would be generally molecular biology, cellular biology, neurobiology, immunology, or genetics. The specific requirements of the individual scientists were not known.

The Institute reviewed the planning options. One approach would be to pursue specialized planning based around individual needs. Not only did the status of recruiting preclude this approach, but specialized planning also carries a unique burden. A specialized laboratory space will undoubtably not meet the needs of the second occupant, either functionally or emotionally. That person will naturally want to change the space to meet their unique wants or needs. The Institute approached the expansion by creating generic space, and then agreeing to tune that space to investigators' needs shortly before they moved in. The Institute approach was to make the facilities standardized enough that they would be adaptable from one investigator to the next with only modest changes. The following is an overview of the planning process used in the Institute expansion.

The generic space approach begins not with individual needs, but rather with what makes a good building. What are the basic components of that building type and what are the amounts and relationships of those components? The goal was to design buildings so that they would be useful in 5 years (at construction completion), as well as in 10 years and beyond. The focus was on the big issues, laboratory modules, support space, office modules, interaction spaces, and circulation systems. The end product was 13 buildings each with a different floor plan, but all of which were based on a common planning approach. The planning goal produced standardized buildings but allowed each to be unique, based on site issues, recruiting philosophy, and university culture.

A number of issues need to be addressed early on in the planning process. The recruitment pattern should be understood. How much space should be given to an assistant professor, an associate professor, and a full professor? The recruitment pattern needs to be tested on potential floor plates as they are developed. Obviously, the smaller floor plate you have, the more difficult it is to have different arrangements. Another issue is the individual components of a laboratory building. A basic starting point is an understanding that a lab building is at best 50% wet laboratory space. The support space should be 35 to 40% or more of the total space, and office space is as little as 10 to 15%. Equally important is trying to understand how a building might need to change over time, and how those changes can be accommodated in any potential plan. Good generic planning processes address these issues throughout the planning process.

The primary component in any biochemistry type laboratory building is the laboratory unit. In 1985, the university standard was a 4 person laboratory of approximately 500 square feet with individual benches, a desk at the end of the benches, and a common sink. The Institute evaluated this model against the proposed recruitment pattern and found that a six-person lab would be a more useful size for the various investigator levels. That size related to the minimum size needed for a high-quality assistant investigator. Various models of the labs were developed for different buildings in response to the recruitment patterns. The models were also tested against the inevitable need to put additional people into the lab. The look at the laboratory unit also made necessary a look at the subcomponents. One overriding issue became apparent. The laboratory unit needed to house not only the individual desks and benches, shared fume hoods and sinks, but also a surprising amount of common equipment. When that space is added to the laboratory module, the unit becomes quite large and the space per person increases. If space is not provided in the lab, it must be provided next to the lab in support spaces. The support space ratio would need to rise equally or exceed the lab space.

The traditional 500-square-foot lab was composed of 8-foot benches, 4-foot desk, an end sink and a fume hood. Each aisle housed two persons. That approach fixed that amount of space per person and made it difficult to change laboratory occupancy without major construction. The Institute tried to take a look at other ways to house people in laboratories. One model located three people on a dead-end aisle with two benches and one desk on one side and a sink, one bench, and two desks on the other side. This approach allowed 3 people per aisle in a 26-foot-deep laboratory module. This approach gave less space per person, but addressed the growing after occupancy concerns. The model was used in three buildings and allowed investigators to adjust the lab occupancy at move in or later. The Institute also developed flexible benchwork systems to support these changes. The benchwork systems allowed the change of function from desk to bench and back without great cost or difficulty. The benchwork systems also allow the relocation of undercounter cabinetry without affecting the top or service systems.

The laboratory size should follow the recruitment pattern, but one should also be aware of how to increase the space assignment as an investigator matures. The arrangement of laboratories in relation to each other will dictate how easily a building can be reassigned. One approach for easy reassignment is the open laboratory. An investigative group could change size without moving walls. When these labs are multiply assigned, they often become chaotic because no one person is in charge. On the other hand, open labs function very well for large investigative groups where one person is in charge. Open labs often produce interesting boundary disputes not present when walls separate space assignments. Another way to think about labs is to have them as individual units that are interconnected. It makes sense to gang labs together in a manner that will accommodate future changes in space assignments. The ganging allows internal circulation, creating what is called a ghost corridor. Assignments can be changed by opening or closing doors. Both patterns were explored in the Institute's expansion.

The office component, though minor in overall percentage, has traditionally had a strong relationship to the laboratory unit. That means it was next to or included in the laboratory unit. Most investigators are familiar with this model and prefer it. The relationship should not to be readily ignored. Having the investigator close, especially at the assistant level, is beneficial to the lab group. The opposite model places offices in groups to promote interaction among investigators. This model allows for ganged laboratory space. A building will have a significantly different floor plan depending on the model chosen. A third model was explored by the Institute. That model placed small groups of offices at the ends of lab banks to create an intimate office-to-lab relationship. The banks of lab space were sufficiently large to allow for changes in assignments without relocation of other components. The location of the offices will likely reflect the culture of the institution that one is dealing with.

The biggest issue affecting lab buildings over the past 15 to 20 years is equipment. Equipment can be housed both on the floor and on the bench top. Miniaturization has moved much equipment out of specialized environments and to the benchtop. Early research buildings had only labs and offices. In the 60s, the need for equipment space arose and affected the order of laboratory buildings. Support space became a necessity, both inside the lab for equipment, and adjacent to or near the labs to house the specialized equipment. Additionally, some specialized environmental areas were also required. The impact of equipment has been felt on the residual amount of available wet biochemistry type laboratory space. Lab support space continues to grow, affecting the amount of standard lab space. If one does not talk about support space early on, a building will be created that will need extensive construction at move in.

There are various kinds of support space. Some of the space is allocated to fixed rooms that are not likely to change, such as cold rooms, dark rooms, and glass washrooms. There will also be support rooms that house common equipment or shared equipment for several investigators. These spaces need to be very highly serviced spaces with air handling, plumbing, and electrical services. They allow the isolation of noisy and heat-producing equipment. Other spaces are also needed for tissue culture, special procedure, fluorescent microscopy, etc. All belong in specialized or isolated environments. When you start to plan a building five years before occupancy, that equipment is usually not known and often not even developed. The key is trying to predict the amount of space that will be required or conversely developing a model that allows the amount of support space to change without extensive construction. The latter model has also been successfully explored by the Institute.

When you are planning a building, you want to have enough laboratory support space so no matter how you assign the building, you have enough of it to adequately support the people. If the floor plate is not big enough, one investigator with peculiar needs can use all the support space and really make it difficult to house other people. A large floor plate size of 15,000 to 16,000 net will help mitigate the impact of one peculiar set of individual requirements. The larger size also allows more interaction by having more people assigned to a floor. Predicting the appropriate amount of support space and having a large enough floor plate are key ingredients to a smooth occupancy process.

The last major issue, especially in academic buildings, is the issue of interaction. Interaction in older buildings occurred in the halls and around blackboards. If you were not in your lab, you had a chance of meeting someone out in the hallways. Today, there is a need to get food out of the laboratories. Places for coffee breaks and lunches are a necessity. These places, if appropriately located and protected from encroachment, also provide a potential for interaction. Open modules promote interaction. The spaces should be accessible and usable. They should encourage the 5- and 10-minute break without forcing one off the floor, promoting casual interaction among different laboratory groups.

A good generic laboratory planning process begins with discussions of how buildings will work in the future. The discussions focus on what makes a good and adaptable laboratory building, which can house a variety of functions in an orderly manner. The focus on the larger planning issues versus individual needs has produced very interesting buildings. Great care also should be taken to understand how buildings will be occupied and what changes will occur then. Good planners are obligated to continually observe the move-in and change process so that necessary accommodations can be made in the generic models. The process should end with a unique plan that can be adapted for present and future uses.

Current State of the Art in Research Facility Design

An Architect's Viewpoint

LEEVI KIIL

Haines Lundberg Waehler
115 Fifth Avenue
New York, New York 10003

My purpose is to discuss the process of how the architectural profession, working with the scientific community and the building industry, is developing research facilities to produce buildings that anticipate the future. The future is embedded in the buildings that we are designing today. We talked about the fact that many of the laboratory buildings that we occupy, particularly on university campuses, are more than 50 years old, and some probably more than 100 years old. So the science buildings that we design and build today really have to endure and must be capable of changing as science and technology advance.

We refer to how science is changing very rapidly. Over the last decade, architects have heard that message clearly. As a profession, we have tried to incorporate the kind of flexibility into our buildings that will support adaptability and change. But, while science and technology are advancing very rapidly, the building industry advances very slowly. The traditional methods of building have been around for decades, if not centuries. And they are likely to stay the same for a long time to come.

Engineering systems have driven many of the technological changes that are happening in buildings, and many of these are positive. But the "bricks and mortar" will still be with us in the foreseeable future. The real issue that we as architects and engineers and the building team have to deal with is: how can the research buildings that we put up now endure over the next half century and deal with what may be out there in the year 2050?

I believe the real answer to that challenge is that our buildings should not compete with the scientists they house. Our buildings should support and enhance the scientific process, but not compete with it. We will find from some of the examples that I will discuss, that when the buildings begin to compete and the designs try to make too much of a statement of their own, it gets in the way of the activities that were intended for the buildings. The title of this talk reflects that this is *an* architect's viewpoint because I do not consider myself as having the singular position on these issues. The projects

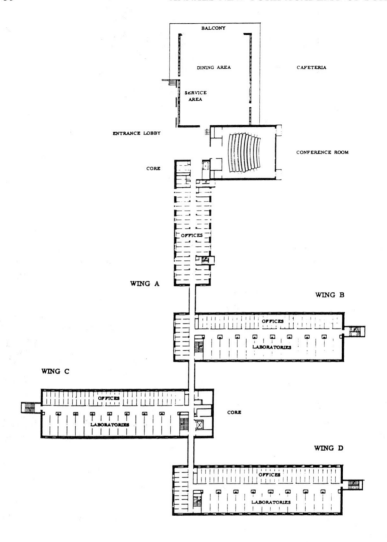

PLAN AT LEVEL 1

FIGURE 1. Koppers Research Center. First floor plan. Voorhees Walker Smith Smith Architects.

that I will discuss are not all mine. But I have chosen a variety of things to stimulate the thinking of the audience.

Let us consider some lessons learned from facilities that were designed in the 50s and 60s, and perhaps look at the Koppers Research Center (FIG. 1), which was thought to incorporate a good deal of flexibility. The scheme created a lot of repetitive lab modules. On an individual basis, those lab modules had every possible service and utility capability within them. But this alone no longer meets the requirements of a good research building as we see it today. As a result of the attenuated configuration, staff are extremely spread out and probably very little interaction occurs. I think the object lesson of this particular facility is to learn from the mistakes that were made in the past–unnecessary redundancy of services, absence of a critical mass of shared space–and try not to repeat them.

The Salk Institute (FIG. 2), designed by Louis Kahn, is a building that was built 30 years ago. Conversely, it has functioned and adapted a lot better than the previous example. Part of the vision behind this building was to invest a degree of flexibility into the design and particularly into the facility's infrastructure. It was this flexibility, together with extraordinary siting and design rigor, that has allowed Salk to endure so well and so powerfully. Two facilities from the sixties, but two dramatically different results.

As architects and scientists, as we undertake a project process, we must cope with the conflicts that are an inherent aspect of research facilities (FIG. 3). It is a building type that continually reflects the struggle between freedom and control.

First is the *technological and the human conflict.* There is an inherent conflict between the mechanistic nature of a technological lab environment and the humanistic needs of the people who occupy it. We are constrained in making labs as humanistic as we would like. So, the buildings have to compensate in some way, providing softer spaces in places outside of the laboratory.

Second, there is the issue of *specificity versus flexibility*–the struggle between planning labs as generic spaces to meet a variety of disciplines versus customizing labs for specific individuals.

The third is the issue of *isolation versus openness.* I think science as a discipline wants to be open because collaboration and the sharing of ideas are very important to the scientific process. Yet, there are reasons why specific activities must be isolated within a research facility. There are the compelling issues of safety, security, and containment either to protect the outside world or to protect a particular experiment.

Finally, there is the *dynamism of the scientific process, which is advancing and rapidly changing, versus the static nature of the building itself.* Developing compatibility between these two forces is a major challenge of research facility design.

I will discuss several buildings that deal with these conflicting issues and influences. FIGURE 4 lists several issues that we commonly deal with in research facility design. None are any great surprise to those of us who are familiar with the design of research facilities. I will deal with some of these

FIGURE 2. Salk Institute for Biological Studies. La Jolla, California—1962. Louis Kahn, Architect.

- Technological vs. Human
- Specificity vs. Flexibility
- Isolation vs. Openness
- Dynamics of Science vs. Static Building Industry

FIGURE 3. Conflicts inherent in research facility design.

issues in the context of how several specific projects have been influenced or how they have responded.

If there is one thing that should be emphasized, it is the issue of space. It is the most important need in any research facility. Most projects have been driven by the lack of space. Research facility space is expensive, costing probably upwards of $250 a square foot in the Northeast. As facility designers, planners, and scientists, we have to strategize our designs so that we can squeeze out as much space as possible. The other part of that issue is that while space is valuable in a building, in a research facility, only about half of it is really usable. The net to gross ratios in research facilities are about 50% to a maximum of 60% usable by the scientists. The remainder that is not directly usable is the infrastructure that makes the building function as a laboratory–mechanical, electrical, and plumbing systems, corridors, and circulation systems.

- Space
- Flexibility and Adaptability
- Pathways to Accommodate Technological Change
- Office Space
- Support and Equipment Space
- Environmental Controls
- Support Communications and Team Dynamics
- Researcher Friendly
- Maintenance Friendly
- Cost Effective/Value Based/More with Less

FIGURE 4. Key needs in research facilities.

I think we will see that in the future more space per individual will be required in research facilities, but driven, as others have noted, not by people but by more equipment. We see in the research that we have done that there will be an overall increase in the total amount of space that we will have to provide in our research facilities per person. And yet, economic pressures are forcing us to constrain space growth so that we can achieve buildings that are as cost effective as possible.

FIGURE 5 illustrates an advanced technology center at the University of Iowa, which was designed by Frank Gehry. It is a very sculptural building with an evocative and definite expression. One can certainly react to that either positively or negatively in whether that is going to work for a scientist. But if you look at the floor plan (FIG. 6), I think that this building has dealt with the laboratory space intelligently. It is all grouped together in one large area of the building, with other non laboratory spaces grouped elsewhere. These other spaces create the building's sculptural quality. But the lab space itself is really just a large rectangular box, designed fairly flexibly.

One of the key elements that we as designers try to achieve is to try to get the buildings as deep as possible, to make the laboratory portions of the building deep enough so that flexible amounts of laboratory space can be created. The expressions can be vastly different, and those are other influences that architects bring to a project. But, again, the laboratory space is grouped together in large blocks and is designed in a way that can be changed over the next several decades.

Here is another example. The Schering-Plough Pharmaceutical Development Facility building designed by HLW (FIG. 7) is a process research facility and contains some manufacturing within it. The overall floor plate is about the size of a football field. The driving idea was to eliminate from the central block of space as much of the vertical elements as possible and allow the freedom to revise the floor plan in practically any way desirable. This is at least one intelligent way of dealing with the need to be able to change later.

A fundamental characteristic of good laboratory buildings no matter what the exterior might look like is that a large flexible field of space is dedicated to laboratories.

The other spatial issue is how you put it all together. The next example is a very large facility of about a million square feet that we just recently designed (the Schering-Plough Research Institute Drug Discovery Facility, FIG. 8). Dealing with such a large amount of space, assembling it in sizable laboratory blocks, but not overwhelming the occupants with its size and magnitude, was critical to achieving a successful design. Woven into that configuration are not only the laboratories but the managerial offices as well, which have been placed to give the office space accessibility to the labs in the five laboratory blocks.

FIGURE 5. Iowa Advanced Technology Laboratories (IATL). Iowa City, Iowa—1993. Frank O. Gehry and Assoc., Architects. (Photo courtesy of Erich Ansel Koyama.)

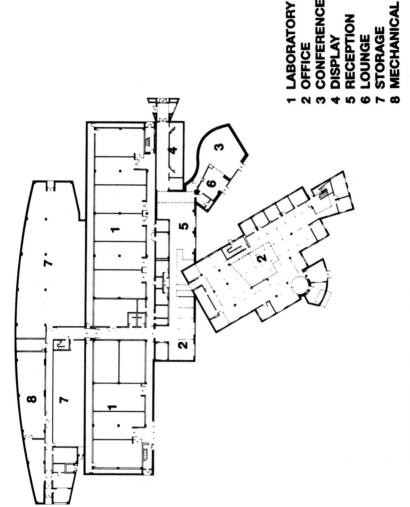

1 LABORATORY
2 OFFICE
3 CONFERENCE
4 DISPLAY
5 RECEPTION
6 LOUNGE
7 STORAGE
8 MECHANICAL

FIGURE 6. Ground floor plan: IATL. (Drawing courtesy of Frank O. Gehry and Assoc.)

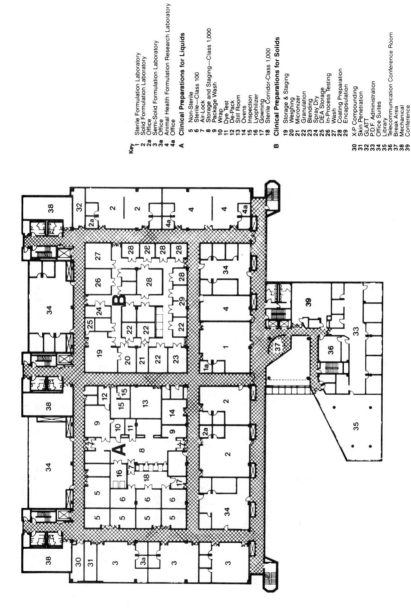

Key

1 Sterile Formulation Laboratory
2 Solid Formulation Laboratory
2a Office
3 Semi-Solid Formulation Laboratory
3a Office
4 Animal Health Formulation Research Laboratory
4a Office

A Clinical Preparations for Liquids

5 Non-Sterile
6 Sterile—Class 100
7 Air-Lock
8 Storage and Staging—Class 1,000
9 Package Wash
10 Wrap
11 Dye Test
12 De-Pack
13 Still Room
14 Ovens
15 Inspection
16 Lyophilizer
17 Gowning
18 Sterile Corridor-Class 1,000

B Clinical Preparations for Solids

19 Storage & Staging
20 Weighing
21 Micronizer
22 Granulation
23 Blending
24 Spray Dry
25 DEA Storage
26 In-Process Testing
27 Wash
28 Coating Preparation
29 Encapsulation

30 X-P Compounding
31 Skin Penetration
32 GLATT
33 P.D.F. Administration
34 Office Suites
35 Library
36 Telecommunication Conference Room
37 Break Area
38 Mechanical
39 Conference

FIGURE 7. Second floor plan: Schering-Plough Research Institute (SPRI) Pharmaceutical Development Facility (PDF). Kenilworth, NJ–1986. Haines Lundberg Waehler, Architects and Engineers. Clinical manufacturing areas are in the center of the floor.

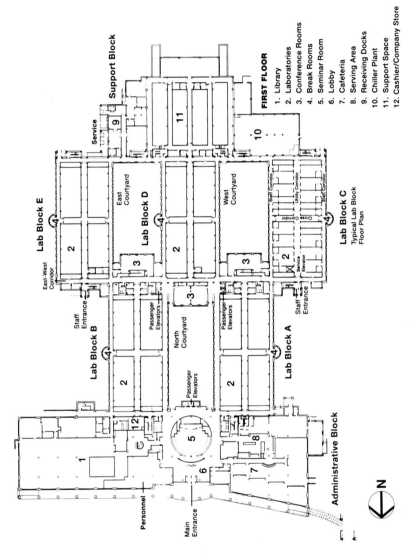

FIRST FLOOR

1. Library
2. Laboratories
3. Conference Rooms
4. Break Rooms
5. Seminar Room
6. Lobby
7. Cafeteria
8. Serving Area
9. Receiving Docks
10. Chiller Plant
11. Support Space
12. Cashier/Company Store

FIGURE 8. First floor plan: Schering-Plough Research Institute (SPRI) Drug Discovery Facility (DDF). Kenilworth, NJ–1992. Haines Lundberg Waehler, Architects and Engineers.

FIGURE 9 illustrates the lab suite, the building block that generated the design. This lab suite provides the capability of proportioning the laboratory, the office, and the support space in various different combinations. It is basically three laboratory modules about 35 feet deep. The space within can be any combination of laboratory, office, or support space. Often scientists prefer exterior views from the laboratories or offices. In this instance you do not get that. Rather, you get a public corridor on one side and a service corridor on the other. This is one of the compromises that must be accepted in order to get the kind of extensive flexibility that this layout offers. And I think there are always such compromises that architect and scientist have to discuss together and see which are the highest priorities.

Creating pathways within the buildings to deal with the delivery of the multitude of services and engineering systems required to conduct research is a major aspect for both technical adequacy and flexibility. This is accomplished in numerous ways. One approach is to sandwich levels of utilities in between the laboratory floors. These interstitial floors (FIGS. 10 and 11) give the freedom to maintenance crews to maintain, repair, and change mechanical systems without disturbing the labs or the occupants.

Another method is the use of service corridors (FIG. 12). These are corridors that run in between laboratories and allow the grouping of all service elements, duct work, electrical cabling, and panels serving the labs. This kind of a corridor can also serve as a place for the movement of supplies and waste materials independent of the general traffic within the building.

These pathways are very important in laboratory facilities. How they are dealt with to support both the flexibility and operational objectives of the research program is one of the key determinants of how successful a laboratory will be. The structuring of these pathways, the architecture of the distribution systems, is a major driver of the building's basic design and configuration.

Another consideration is the pervasiveness of environmental concerns and environmental sensitivity in shaping and driving projects. Environmental issues for research facilities now consume enormous amounts of time and attention on the part of designers. This is a site plan of the Schering-Plough Research site in Kenilworth, New Jersey (FIG. 13). One of the telling illustrations about this site is in the flood plain map (FIG. 14) which shows in hatching the areas that have been categorized as a flood plain by the state. Five years ago, the flood plain area was far less than it is today. Through increased stringency and changes in environmental regulations, very little land was left to accommodate the new projects. This will probably happen throughout the country. As a result, we are dealing with less land and with tighter regulations, which will affect the way designers and the building team do their work.

Often there is a dizzying number of overlapping jurisdictions to cope with. This map (FIG. 15) shows some of the jurisdictions that we dealt with for the Schering-Plough project from federal to state to the local municipality

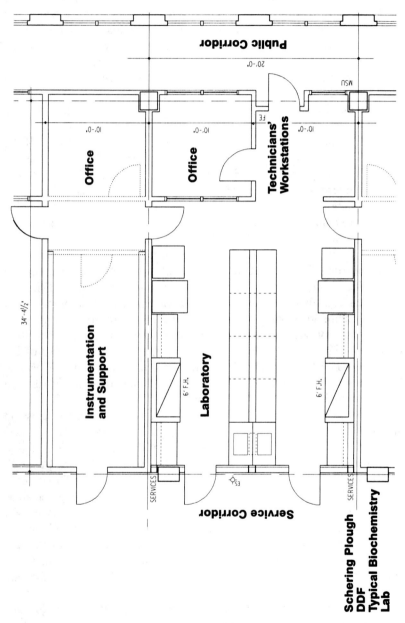

FIGURE 9. Lab suite: SPRI DDF.

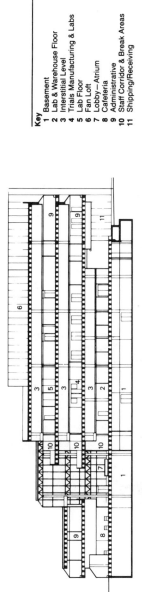

Key
1 Basement
2 Lab & Warehouse Floor
3 Interstitial Level
4 Trials Manufacturing & Labs
5 Lab Floor
6 Fan Loft
7 Lobby—Atrium
8 Cafeteria
9 Administrative
10 Staff Corridor & Break Areas
11 Shipping/Receiving

FIGURE 10. Building section: SPRI PDF. This section illustrates operating floors and interstitial floors.

FIGURE 11. Interstitial floor: SPRI PDF.

FIGURE 12. Utility corridor: SPRI DDF.

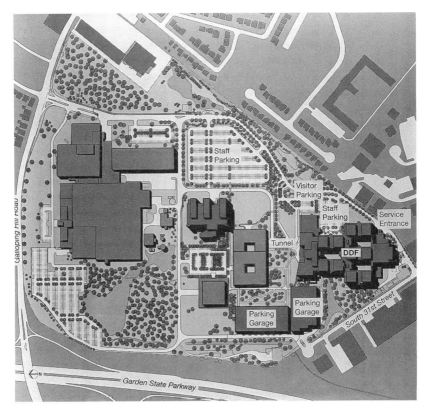

FIGURE 13. Site plan: Schering-Plough, Kenilworth, NJ. The DDF is on the right, the PDF is in the center.

itself. This trail of activity became a project in itself. It ran from the earliest stages of design through to the end of construction activity.

In the future, we will also have to deal with recycling older sites because of the difficulties of vacating sites that companies and institutions have lived in for many years. As designers, we have to create ways for them to recycle those sites, adapt them to the future, make them more environmentally sensitive, and take advantage of their real estate.

I would like to return for a moment to the issues of humanizing the research environment. A growing demand of researchers is to have a supportive and productive work environment. One issue is the human need for daylight. Whether buildings have narrow floor plans or have large amounts of interior space, we need to employ strategies to introduce daylight into the buildings.

Human scale is another aspect of humanization. The Genetics Institute in Cambridge, MA, designed by Payette Assoc., has got a very nice, very

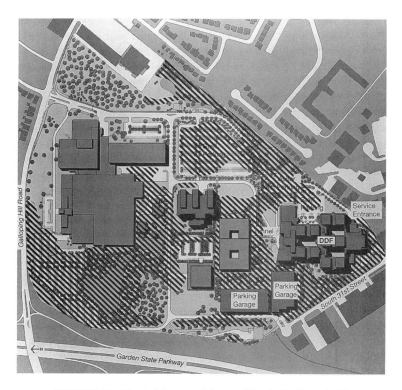

FIGURE 14. Flood plain map: Schering-Plough, Kenilworth, NJ.

comfortable human scale (FIG. 16). It is a two story building with an internal staircase that allows people to interact and intercommunicate within the building without having to go into an isolated elevator. The airy, open quality and its warmth contribute to its role as a centralizing element in this facility.

The nature of the particular site also has great relevance to the building design. What type of campus the building is located on and what those neighboring buildings are like define our particular buildings' responsibility to that campus. This project, which we designed on the University of Mississippi campus, is a highly sophisticated technological building dedicated to research in physical acoustics (FIG. 17). It has a very large open field of laboratory space. On the outside, offices ring the entire space. The laboratories (FIG. 18) had to be internal because of the need to impose stringent control over the environment within the laboratory. The exterior of the building adapted a classical style of architecture to respond to the campus environment (FIG. 19). The University of Mississippi project is as technologically sophisticated as any building that we have talked about and seen, but the exterior has to

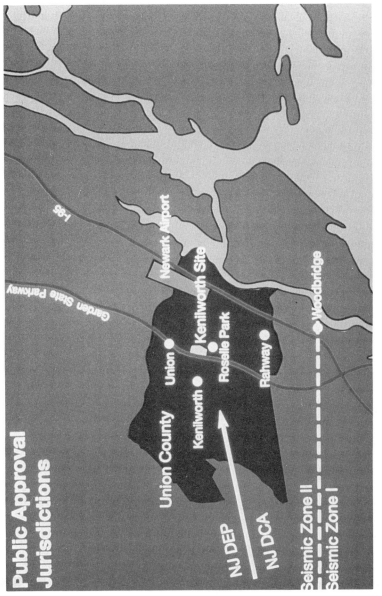

FIGURE 15. Jurisdictions map: Schering-Plough, Kenilworth, NJ.

FIGURE 16. Atrium and central meeting area: Genetics Institute. Cambridge, MA—ca. 1986. (Photo courtesy Payette & Assoc., Architects.)

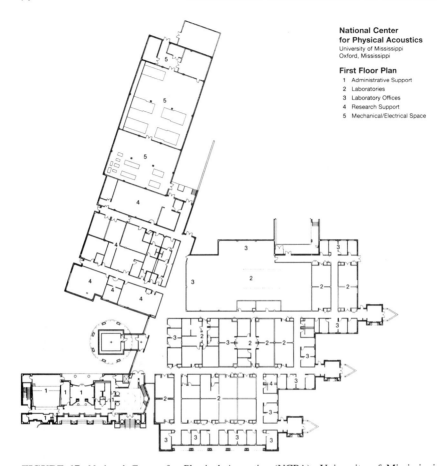

**National Center
for Physical Acoustics**
University of Mississippi
Oxford, Mississippi

First Floor Plan

1 Administrative Support
2 Laboratories
3 Laboratory Offices
4 Research Support
5 Mechanical/Electrical Space

FIGURE 17. National Center for Physical Acoustics (NCPA)–University of Mississippi. Oxford, Miss.–1990. Haines Lundberg Waehler/Mockee Coker Tumer, Architects and Engineers.

respond to the more permanent and enduring values of that setting. The interior and the exterior of that building are vastly different. Frequently, this division of responsibilities between the internal users and the external community is an issue we as designers must deal with.

As a final point, I want to touch on the issue of cost effectiveness and how we can build that into our facilities and deal with the pressures of funding. The AgBiotech Facility (Foran Hall) we have just designed for Rutgers (Fig. 20), is interesting because the funding was anticipated to come from several different federal and state sources possibly over different time periods. We created a design for the building that essentially allowed the building to be taken apart in the event that any of those funding sources did

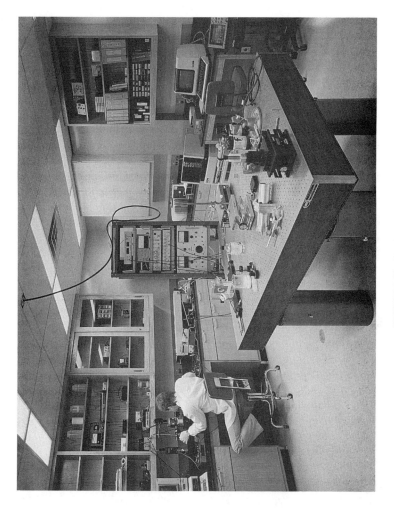

FIGURE 18. Typical lab: NCPA.

FIGURE 19. Building exterior: NCPA. The building's design exhibits the Georgian influence of the campus architecture.

FIGURE 20. Rutgers AgBiotech Center/Walter Foran Hall. New Brunswick, NJ—est. completion 1994. Haines Lundberg Waehler, Architects and Engineers.

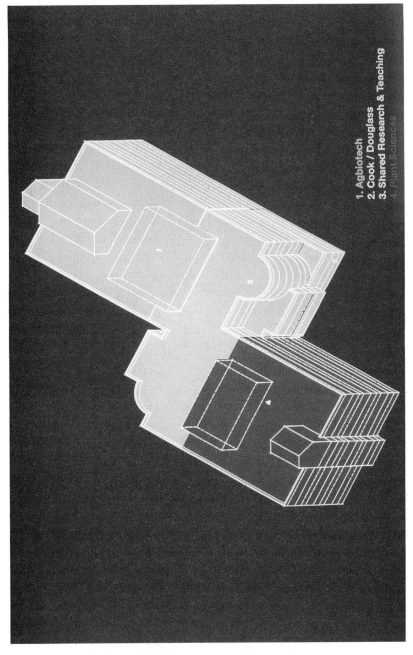

FIGURE 21. Segments of AgBiotech keyed to funding source.

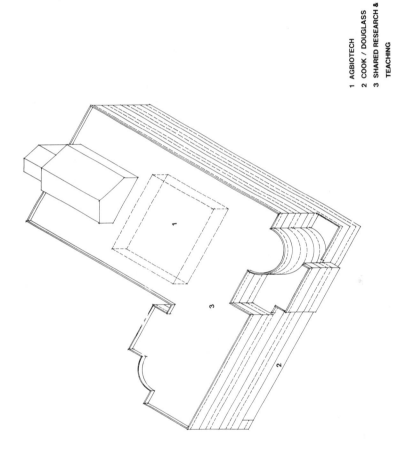

1 AGBIOTECH
2 COOK / DOUGLASS
3 SHARED RESEARCH &
 TEACHING

FIGURE 22. AgBiotech scope reduction scenario. Reduction scenario with one wing removed.

not materialize (Fig. 21). We adopted a jigsaw puzzle approach. The building was designed to be demountable so that if at the time when final design began, it looked as if those funding sources were not about to happen, the unfunded portion could be eliminated from the project (Fig. 22).

We also created a strategy later on in the design process for how we could build as much of the building in the form of shell space so that if the project went over budget, or if the funding could not be realized, we could at least build the shell space and then fit it out later. Again I return almost full circle to the issue of space as having the utmost importance. Once you have the space, it is easy to do something with it. And, it is easier if you have shell space to find money to fit out particular laboratories than to try to add a whole portion to a building. Fortunately on this project, most of the funding did come through as anticipated so we did not have to take the jigsaw puzzle apart. In fact a lot of the shell space is being fit out now, so I think there is good news there; because of the competitiveness of the economy, we are able to do that. But this is just an example of the kinds of strategies that include both foresight and defensiveness that we have to work out together–scientists, facilities staffs, architects, and engineers–so that we can get these buildings built in an environment of economic competitiveness and constraint. I think these kinds of pressures will probably get more intense as we go into the 90s and perhaps beyond.

The future is embedded in our current designs because, with every decision, we make a commitment to some aspect of the future. Cost effectiveness is a good place to end because it returns me full circle to a fundamental role of the architect: to make certain that your investment in a research facility, whether it be in space, flexibility, utility, distribution pathways, or supportive humanizing features, has been made with enough foresight to accommodate future changes.

The Issues of Lab Design and Current State of the Art

An Engineer's Viewpoint

TIMOTHY D. BAKER

R. G. Vanderweil Engineers, Inc.
266 Summer Street
Boston, Massachusetts 02210-1112

This presentation is a discussion of the MEP (mechanical, electrical, and plumbing services) engineer's role and responsibility in the design of present day state of the art research and development facilities, and a positive example of how communication of the design intent to the O&M (operations and maintenance) staff is crucial to the successful long-term economical operation of the lab service systems. First, what is an MEP engineer and why is what we do important to an R&D facility project?

To put what we do into context, the MEP consultant provides the design for all of the building and science support systems. These include the automatic temperature control and the equipment and auxiliaries for building and process cooling and heating, the ventilation air, exhaust facilities, water, and electricity. Lab services such as compressed air, vacuum, specialty gas distribution for argon, oxygen, nitrogen, etc., pure water, drains and vents for domestic and acid waste, etc., are all included. This paper uses the broad topics of air, water, and electricity in the discussion.

Air is the breath of any R&D facilities project. Without it, safe science cannot proceed. The circulation/ventilation air for cooling and heating transport, fume exhaust, odor and particulate control and aerosol pressurization, and make-up supply air for air flow barrier and/or containment uses are all a part of a successful "air" system in the R&D setting.

The water systems we design and distribute provide a consistent, ever-present base for experimentation for solvent/dilution service, for glassware and equipment washing and in pure water heating and distillation all the way from sterilization and bio-kill applications to WFI, water for injection.

As a silent partner, electricity for illumination and power both in the lab and behind the scenes for air and water transport. Electrical distribution systems for uninterrupted power supplies for critical computer instrumentation, for voice and data transmission, and for life safety alarm and notification.

Again–context, cost and space, the systems we design require expenditures of between 40 to 45 cents out of every R&D facility construction dollar.

TABLE 1. Systems Cost for Research Facilities[a]

Excavation, foundation & structure	24.73	31.25	32.88	40.61
Exterior envelope	12.39	20.28	20.15	26.81
Interior construction and finishes	20.88	24.51	26.17	34.89
Specialties & equipment	15.51	21.79	23.64	38.83
Conveying systems	1.24	3.18	2.97	4.65
Plumbing	15.40	20.92	20.71	25.61
Fire protection	1.94	3.08	3.58	8.22
HVAC & controls	43.90	54.22	59.67	112.17
Electrical	15.74	23.77	25.96	39.60
Subtotal–MEP	76.98	101.99	109.92	185.60
TOTAL–all work	151.73	203.00	215.73	331.39
Percent–MEP	50.7%	50.2%	51.0%	56.0%

[a] Taken from Historical Cost Data, a national general contractor, presented to the R&D Laboratory Design Seminar for the International Society for Pharmaceutical Engineering.

Specific *lab only* buildings often require a higher percentage of the cost, sometimes over 50¢ of each of the total project construction dollars. That portion for MEP services for lab only projects is tabulated in TABLE 1.

As a spatial concern, we need large and vertically and horizontally contiguous spaces to house our equipment and systems, as well as housing the ductwork, piping, cable trays and electrical bus duct throughout the buildings. Unfortunately, we negatively contribute to some of the least efficient construction types in our business. Labs often are 55% or less efficient; this is important–this means that for every 55 square feet of net usable lab space, the R&D owner must build 100 square feet of building. The missing 45 square feet of space goes to cores and vertical transportation as is typical for all construction *and* a full extra measure to house our extraordinary equipment, ductwork, and cable.

What elements are included in "state of the art" labs? In the order of air, water, and electricity, the following MEP work would be present in the typical R&D project.

Ventilation Systems

Merely adequate ventilation in an R&D setting is not acceptable. Building local and national codes and guidelines provide recommended environmental conditions for lab spaces; these spaces are temperature and humidity regulated and require close tolerances, especially those that house laboratory animals.

TABLE 2

	Relative	Dry-Bulb Temperature[a]	
Mouse	40-70	18-26	64.4-78.8
Rat	40-70	18-26	64.4-78.8
Hamster	40-70	18-26	64.4-78.8
Guinea pig	40-70	18-26	64.4-78.8
Rabbit	40-60	16-21	60.8-69.8
Cat	30-70	18-29	64.4-84.2
Dog	30-70	18-29	64.4-84.2[b]
Nonhuman primate	30-70[c]	18-29	64.4-84.2
Chicken	45-70	17-27	60.8-80.6[d]

[a] From ILAR, 1965, 1966, 1973a, 1978a,b, 1980.

[b] Temperature of 27-29 °C (80.6-84.2 °F) recommended in post-operative recovery.

[c] Recommended range of 60%-65% for marmosets, tamarins, owl monkeys.

[d] Recommendations for chickens 6 weeks of age or older.

TABLE 2 is taken from *The Guide for the Care and Use of Laboratory Animals,* a National Institutes of Health publication. Notice the dry bulb temperature range for rabbits. When we keep rabbit colonies within a building typically designed for indoor temperatures for humans, the humans require comfort ranges usually always between 72 ° and 75 °F. In order to satisfy the 60.8-69.8 °F range, the bunny rooms or suites must be fitted with an additional series of recool coils that use the filtered building ventilation air, subcool it additionally by chilled water systems, and send it to the colony. All of this air is one pass supply, then immediately exhausted at the rate of once every four minutes all day long, forever.

In the biology, molecular biology, and life sciences fields, thousands of laboratory animals are nurtured, housed, and used in everyday experimentation. Environmental air systems for odor and vapor removal are essential to the life and well being of the colony. The most outstanding R&D operators concern themselves not only with survivability issues, but also those that enhance the quality of life of their colonies. Being aware of the current national political and social climate as it relates to the importance of the use of animals in research, most R&D communities already maintain animal breeding and nursery facilities for nonhuman primates and other specialty colonies.

Beyond the animal area, ventilation air is used in essentially every module within the lab. The air is supplied to "makeup," i.e., replenish, that which becomes contaminated within the lab and consequently must be removed by the laboratory equipment like fume hoods, wash area hoods, and bio cabinets.

Air transport and air supply and exhaust systems are the primary engineering system in the R&D building–without it, the control of the interior environment becomes erratic, overcooled, or overheated and immediately contaminated.

State of the art R&D facilities use an enormous amount of air. A typical module with one or more fume hoods requires between 20 and 40 air changes every hour, i.e., one complete air supply and exhaust of the total volume every two minutes. In a building like the Environmental Protection Agencies Research Center in Raleigh, North Carolina we are using 1,100,000 cubic feet of outdoor supply air every minute. This amount calculates to 1,100,000 ft^3/min × 60 min/h × 24 h/day × 0.073 pounds/ft^3 = 115,632,000 pounds of air/day, and this is "typical" of these major R&D facilities. With the supply is a similarly sized exhaust/air removal system. Just to transport this air quantity, more than one thousand two hundred horsepower of fan force is needed for continuous around the clock, on-line duty.

To circulate this air, we not only need to exhaust it, i.e., draw it from the exhaust site in the lab and via the exhaust fan dump it outdoors, but we also have to make up this loss. Supply air systems in the R&D setting draw in the air, prefilter and final filter it, take it through a state of heat recovery, heat it, humidify it, then via fan arrangements increase its total pressure. The air is then cooled and dehumidified in the summer, and then, via medium to high velocity distribution systems, circulated to every space in the project. State of the art labs need to be "green" facilities since indoor air quality is one of the most important environmental factors in the project.

The automatic temperature controls of the air side system differentiate today's labs from older R&D spaces. We have today the capability of operating "smart" labs where each zone, space, or module is capable of an addressable individual temperature and humidity control set point. The smart controls directing digital microprocessor based network are fiber optic backed with local and master DGPs (data-gathering panels). Each addressable zone is capable of being monitored and reset manually or automatically, and each via software operation can respond to historic preaction, optimization, and alarm and "out of spec" notifications.

Finally, pressure control–in today's state of the art lab, pressure controls and pressure differentials for barrier and/or containment keep the laboratory safe. In BSL-2 (biosafety level 2) facilities–this is typical in biology and molecular biology–the exposure science is done within fume hoods. In BSL-3 projects, fume hoods and bio safety cabinets are required and a higher degree of containment pressurization and monitoring is necessary as the potential threat to the scientists may be airborne. Thus lab air always moves from clean to dirty, less involved to exhaust site, and positive pressure to lower pressure. Not always positive to negative–in the case of SPF mice (specific pathogen free colonies), the colony is protected by a positive air barrier then the surroundings are protected via a series of air locks.

The cooling and heating apparatus that supports the ventilation system in the modern lab is similarly as sophisticated as are the supply systems they serve. Large chillers and boilers supply the heat rejection in summer and outdoor make up air heating in the winter. Laboratories consume 300 to 400 thousand of BTUs per square foot per year, a figure 6 to 8 times that of a modern office building and, today, exceeding even that used in a modern hospital.

The end of the line for air systems in the lab building occurs at the discharge of the exhaust fan. These discharges propel the exhaust air stream out of the reentrainment zone of a building. In some cases, the exhaust has already been prefiltered with roughing filters, especially in animal areas, and activated carbon filtration for radioisotope hoods. At the biomedical research tower at the University of Alabama, we have a BSL-3 animal containment AIDS facility. The exhaust system for this area is barrier, DDC controlled, express ducted to the tenth floor, fitted with nuclear grade "bag in-bag out" filters and pneuma exhaust valves prior to entering the duplex exhaust fan systems, each provided with standby power so that power is never lost to the fans.

Water Systems

The state of the art research laboratory uses substantial water on a 24-hour-a-day basis. Modern labs include systems for domestic use, for "protected" lab uses, for pure water circulation and recirculations, and in production facilities—water for the product and where product is to be injected—water for injection. Water is used as the sterilization medium in nearly every process, heated in stainless steel or glass lined heat exchangers, the water and the product to be sterilized are sustained at a high enough temperature for sufficient duration to be considered safe as ultimately "validated" by the authorities having jurisdiction, often the Food and Drug Administration.

After the "good" things are done with lab water, the effluents, dilutants, solvents, and other waste streams use water as the principal carrying agent. Waste treatment systems in each lab including bio-kill sterilizers need water. In BSL-3 uses, all effluents are sterilized then packaged as hazardous wastes and taken to a hazardous waste incinerator for further reduction and/or sterilization, or incineration.

Water supply and water purification in a lab are complex. A state of the art pure water system contains deionizers, salt tanks, settling chambers, reverse osmosis filtration, sometimes ultraviolet purifiers and circulators and recirculators. The materials that come in contact with the pure water must in themselves not provide any possibility of contamination.

Effluent streams today are regulated to a minor extent when they discharge to a municipal treatment system. As engineers, we must provide temperature regulation such that no waste stream is discharged above a fixed temperature usually, 120 to 140 °F (48.9 to 60 °C). Further, we must provide acid or caustic injection for waste streams to maintain a fixed minimum and maximum discharge pH. Finally, as engineers charged with protecting the public health we must not permit the passage of injurious chemicals, agents, or organisms to be transmitted to the municipal waste stream. Our designs often contain the apparatus for waste treatment including on-line equipment and back-up components in case of failure of the on-line equipment.

Electrical Power

In context, a modern "smart" office building "demands" electrical use on the order of 5 watts per square foot usually peaking for a single 15-minute period each month along with the air conditioning load. The state of the art R&D facility demands much more. It is not unusual for a major facility to pay a million dollar electricity bill each month.

State of the art labs use low voltage power for uses today and equipment not dreamed of even 10 years ago. We regularly today deal with issues in the lab like UPS for computer and conditioned power for instrumentation, teleconferencing centers, E-mail, low brightness lighting of video display terminal areas, and standby power for freezer, incubators, trexlers. We work hard to eliminate fault current, grounding problems, and today we deal with EMF, electromagnetic force fields, that, even after five years of investigation by nearly all of the major national power producers, have eluded all of our prospective diagnosis of import or issue. Behind the scenes in the R&D facility we use, control, distribute, and regulate power at higher voltages. It would surprise some visitors to our modern campuses to know that behind the scenes are 100 kV or higher transmission lines and transformation for more than 40 megawatts of power to serve each one million square feet of R&D space.

We use electricity to power large motors for pumps in sizes up to 400 to 500 horsepower each, or larger. We use 4160 V power to operate centrifugal chillers with 3000 horsepower motors, three or four in one location. These motor horsepowers are large enough that we provide engineering studies for the serving utility company to show how best to start them so that the voltage drop that develops because of their starting is not disturbing to the entire power grid.

On site, in today's state of the art lab facility is its own standby power production facility. Modern R&D buildings include areas of use that cannot be without electrical power. The power produced by these standby plants serves critical exhaust systems, animal environmental systems, and all life safety systems. They power the control networks, are self-contained with their own on-site fuel storage, and by law must be energized at least monthly for the life of the facility.

COMMUNICATION OF THE DESIGN INTENT

The planning and design process that goes into a "state of the art" lab facility may encompass a two to three year time period. With technology changes occurring in a much shorter time frame, often many of the elements that make the facility "state of the art" during the design period are passé or obsolete when the design and two to three year construction/move in are complete. For this reason the elements of the MEP systems that define "state of the art" must be flexible and adaptable for change. The MEP engineer uses an approach to the environmental indoor temperature and airside design that we call applied diversity. As an example of this concept, the mechanical design engineer, at the time of the design and with the concurrence of the owner (and often enthusiasm of the architect), only provides a portion of the full capacity of the ventilation system that otherwise would be included to meet the ultimate facility needs.

Studies and practical experience have shown that for large complexes with fume hoods, the buildings become air driven as opposed to being load driven, and that as engineers we can count on at least 20-30% of all exhaust sites in the building to be closed, i.e., unused at any one time. A facility whose air side calculations, because of the fume hood density, may calculate to a 400,000 CFM (cubic feet of air per minute) requirement, may be provided with only 300,000 CFM during initial construction.

With our owners' concurrence, we provide only 70 to 80% of the peak ventilation capacity knowing with a good deal of certainty that enough hoods will be closed or partially used to allow adequate ventilation service to the remainder of the on-line space. The benefits to applied diversity are very real. The diversity allows the owner to reduce his first cost investment in the MEP systems by essentially the amount of the agreed to diversity, i.e., up to 30%. This means 30% less air handling capacity, 30% less chiller and boiler capacity in systems designed for parallel flow, 30% fewer pumps, valves, electrical connections etc.

FIGURE 1 shows the result of an actual test case. The test facility was a 300,000 square foot pharmaceutical research facility in the eastern United States.

But nothing is without some risk. At move-in, the facility O&M staff *must* be *instructed* on the capabilities and the diversity driven limitations of the systems. This makes the O&M staffs a part of the team, which for many is an unusual role. The importance is that should the diversity not actually occur, the O&M staff who work with the system every day must be alert to

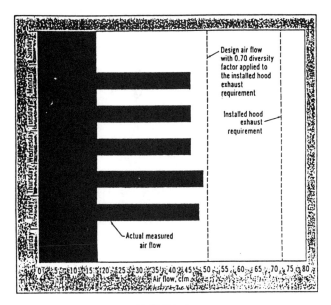

FIGURE 1

when and how to maximize *their* new equipment and at the same time plan for the ''then required'' expansion.

Communication of this level of early planning decisions is the key, when all team members are made aware of the potential risks and benefits, then all team members can with certainty plan for the optimized beneficial use of the engineered capabilities while taking advantage of the natural diversity and the consequent and substantial cost and energy savings.

So our engineer's viewpoint of state of the art is the management and distribution of air, the breath of the R&D facility, water, the life blood of the lab, and electricity, our silent power partner.

Discussion Open to the Floor
Combined with Roundtable

Concerned about global competition and financial pressures, participants from the floor focused on fears about the fallout that would result from change in terms of staff reduction and scope of work resulting from evolving sharing of research programs with others. These issues were then examined in terms of their impact on the use and design of the research and development facility. The difficulty of dealing with uncertainty was a grave concern expressed by the audience.

Responding were the afternoon speakers (Baker, Kiil, Lewis, McGhee) along with Messrs. Cohen and French and Drs. Heintz and Williamson. Stark moderated. They discussed how to make organizational accommodations for change and how architects can help to accommodate the changing scientific environment in which the only thing that is certain is that change will occur. A good deal of time was occupied with discussion of the uncertainty about what science will be conducted in a given space and the way in which equipment has overwhelmed the lab and resulted in space deficiencies in the support areas. It was acknowledged that frequent change has always occurred in laboratory buildings and will increase. The issue is not to allow adaptation and change to become a debilitating factor, but to accept that disruption and cost as inevitable in a building type so dependent on technology, intercommunications, and a variety of delivery systems. In view of this reality, specifics of lab space configuration were discussed along with the inherent tradeoffs. Minimizing disruption requires lots of space in order to create multiple levels of segregation between different functions and circulation systems. This process cannot be cost free.

There was discussion of the need to design for integration of increasing communications technology, not only within the lab, but across the country, and even globally. It was suggested that the real question is how to network, and that decisions will not be made on systems until a life cycle analysis is completed on cost and projected maintenance.

Dr. Lewis acknowledged that bringing together disciplines that originally were individual departments within their own facility introduces enormous organizational and operational issues. He also predicted that we are going to see an explosion of equipment. However, he foresees better use of the vertical space in labs as a new way to accommodate equipment growth.

Drs. Heintz and Lewis stressed a fundamental, even minimalist, view of the basic lab design drivers: an understanding of the process of science in the lab; and a recognition that the design of the lab does not stimulate the

89

creative process of science but is an investment that facilitates the conduct of the scientific process.

Stark predicted that equipment will come with its own furniture. All of the infrastructure ports and the delivery will be there, but there will be fewer fixed elements.

In addition to the expressed need to increase lab support volume, a participant stressed the need for continuing thought being given to corridor design to separate personnel and service. In response to this, Mr. French discussed several alternative schemes and tradeoffs regarding how to get the best separation of people and materials in terms of cost, cautioning, however, that there is no magical solution.

McGhee made the point that he would want to err in favor of the biggest floor plate he could afford and the biggest variety of support spaces possible.

Stark offered the hypothesis that despite management pressures within the research environment to do more with less, the technological and organizational drives are indicating a need for more area per person. The resolution will be that labs will stay about the same size, with all the equipment in a support space for the people who are being pushed out of the lab into a more general and less expensive space. OSHA guidelines are also driving this trend.

In reaction to the perception that mechanical space requirements as a space driver are overgeneralized, Cyrena Simmons of NIH questioned whether system capacity couldn't just be delivered to where you need it.

Timothy Baker agreed that it could be, but at the cost of future flexibility. He pointed out that establishing the balance between system flexibility and system efficiency is a major challenge for facility designers.

Finally, numerous speakers from the audience suggested that, in the light of operating cost pressures, every major design discussion be supported by a life cycle cost analysis.

Opening Remarks Day 2

ALICE S. HUANG

New York University
Washington Square North
New York, New York 10003

As Dean for Science at New York University, I am very much an end user, and as a research scientist, I have also been using laboratories for over 30 years. So maybe, as the Chinese say, if you have enough bowls of rice people will begin to listen to you a little bit.

Many of our ways of thinking about the world and about doing science, as we know it today, really began in the period just following World War II. That is a period when American scientists and academics began to realize that we might indeed be winning the war and that we had some responsibility for the future of what the world would be like. Our ideas about design, construction, and building in some of our research institutions are very refined but we are really still on the same trajectory as in the post-Sputnik era. I do not think we really changed our thinking of how our institutions ought to be. But in the 1990s, much has changed and it is fitting that we reexamine the many assumptions that we have had about doing science and the type of research facilities that scientists will need.

I realize that yesterday there was considerable discussion about some of the possible restrictions or limitations that will come up in the future. But today I think we want to let our imaginations run wild and even open our pocketbooks as wide as possible in thinking what there might be in the future for research facilities and how we can construct something that will truly be functional. To do this I think we should look at our past experience and note those elements in research facilities that were particularly outstanding and worth keeping.

Two of my favorite research facilities for biological science remain the Salk Institute in La Jolla, California, which is not only beautiful but functional, and the Whitehead Institute in Cambridge, Massachusetts. I know that staff from the National University of Singapore came to the Whitehead Institute and liked it so much that they basically took the blueprints (and even the font size for naming ladies' and men's rooms). When I find myself at the Institute of Molecular and Cell Biology in Singapore walking through those corridors, I feel as if I am at the Whitehead Institute. I cannot tell the difference from the inside. It is proof that these successful models travel well. Thus the Salk Institute and the Whitehead Institute are esthetically beautiful workplaces, and both are extremely functional. The supporting infrastructure of the labs provide flexibility. That is a real key.

The ability to adapt to a variety of functional needs for the people working in them is important; in particular the ease to rearrange heating, cooling, electrical, and plumbing support services is a prerequisite of experimental science and was carefully considered. Moreover, thought was given to the quality of the environment so there are pleasant spaces for quiet thinking and sustained work, as well as breakout areas to relax and interact with one's colleagues. At MIT's Whitehead, a percent of the building costs is set aside to provide for artwork, and that has helped to make all of the recently constructed buildings at MIT beautiful both inside and out. So these things—flexibility, esthetics, functionality, and human orientation—are all worthwhile keeping.

For the future we will need, above all, information networks that help to bring colleagues together within a building and also connect them with colleagues and data bases worldwide. Right now, the NYC Economic Development Administration, and some members of a partnership, are considering the development of a building that will be an incubator center for multimedia and software production. In thinking about that building, it is immediately apparent that careful input would be required to insure that this is indeed a functional building. Without such care, I can envision a jumble of wires and cabling running all over.

Electronic communication really needs to be on the most sophisticated level so that scientists in different parts of the world can collaborate at the same time, even on the same experiment, and to work together on the same computer simulation. That is, work together in real time. Perhaps we can think of electronic notebooks for voice input, as well as data input, being easily combined, thus freeing the lab worker from having to put down pipettes in order to write, and from the endless copying of data from one place to another.

These are just some of my wishes. Unfortunately I also see us having to worry more about hazardous waste, safety features, security measures. Newer ways of managing these necessities may alleviate much of the burden of regulatory aspects of running laboratories.

I hope I have gotten your imaginations running and thinking about what your wish lists might turn out to be. I will turn this morning's meeting over to Stanley Stark, Jeffrey French, and Tim Baker, who will try to show us how to get from wishes to realities.

Some Speculations About the Lab of the Future

A Look Ahead

STANLEY STARK

Haines Lundberg Waehler
115 Fifth Avenue
New York, New York 10003

There are five major categories of issues that will promote change in the research facilities of the future:

- Directions of research toward globalized research focuses.

- External political and economic forces that both channel research in particular areas, subject research practice to increased scrutiny, and impose pressure on funding.

- Styles of research activities that will lead to more teamwork, collaboration, flexibility, and intercommunication.

- Market forces that have introduced more competitiveness and have reduced the time available from research start to commercialization.

- Generational change within the research community leading to greater expectations by younger scientific workers of the lab as a quality work environment.

The objective of this paper is to exercise creative speculation to develop some forward thinking about how these issues might influence the design of the research facilities of the future by getting up on our toes and peering over the horizon. The method is to isolate a trend and push it to see if there are physical consequences to the design of the research facility. As I discussed in the introduction, some will be responses to gradual change, some will be non sequiturs, abrupt and without precedent.

This paper combines two related presentations I delivered at the Workshop. The first, "A Palette of Possibilities," was the opening discussion in a series of speculations about the future form of the lab. It was organized to provide a broad view, a random walk through a wide variety of possibilities—internal volatilities, external pressures, and the resulting conflicts.

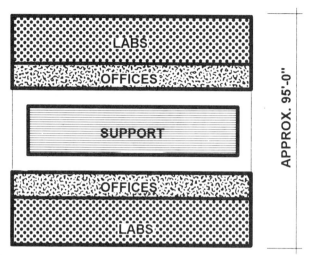

FIGURE 1. Typical current floor plan with lab offices as part of the lab.

The second presentation, "An Architect's View Point: Part II," concentrated on a few external forces, or the external affect of forces, that would change the research facility. "Part I," dealing with the internal pressures of the research community is dealt with in Jeffrey French's paper.

A PALETTE OF POSSIBILITIES

The Pressure to Move People Out of the Lab

Safety and health considerations, new OSHA guidelines related to laboratory safety, the desire for more windows and daylight access, and the steady pressure of increasing amounts of instrumentation are all tending to push office and workstation space for scientists and lab workers out of the laboratory environment. Office space is migrating to the building perimeter adjacent to but separate from the lab and support space environments.

As a result, lab floor plates are likely to get wider. Compare a typical current lab floor plan (FIG. 1) with a version where office and workstation areas are now on the perimeter (FIG. 2). Width has grown from 95 feet to 130 feet, a 37% increase.

Increasing Net Research Area/Person

The net research area per person in lab facilities has been increasing steadily in the 1970s and 1980s. While averages have been between 300 net

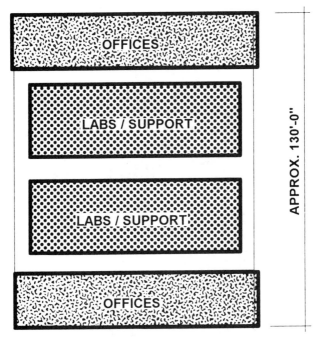

FIGURE 2. Lab floor plan with lab offices on the exterior.

square feet/person-350 net square feet/person throughout that period, this factor is heading toward 400 net square feet/person in the near future (FIG. 3). In the past, the area increases have been driven by technology and utility systems. Now they are being driven by increased amounts of instrumentation and equipment (they are getting smaller but there is a lot more of them), more space for building mechanical systems, more waste-handling provisions, and more accommodations for staff work space and for the support necessary for organizational life. Lab space itself will stay about the same. Support space for equipment and dedicated research functions and office and administrative space for staff will be the major sources of area growth.

There is a contrary view that was also expressed by some members of the audience. This scenario suggests that overall net research area per person will stay the same or will decrease. More area will be devoted to office space, less to lab space. Computerization, automation, sophisticated communication, and control systems will allow more work to be done or controlled remotely from the lab. And labs, which are now territorial and are assigned to individual scientists, will be shared as support space frequently is now. The lab would be an instrument but would no longer serve as a home base.

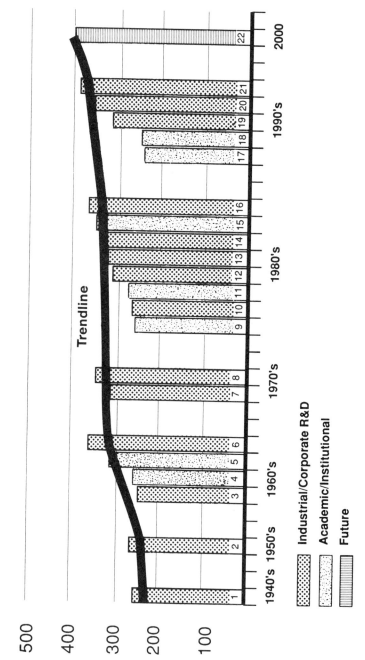

FIGURE 3. Historic trend of net research area/person. The number key represents specific facilities: 1 is Bell Labs; 4 is Salk Institute.

FIGURE 4. Lab building with office space on perimeter and an office building exterior.

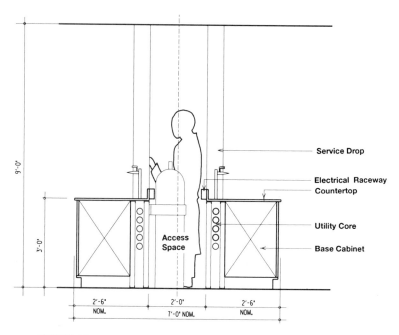

FIGURE 5. Split lab bench. Provides service aisle for instrumentation.

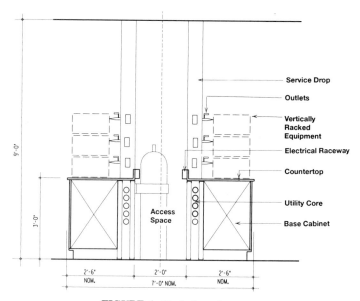

FIGURE 6. Vertical service array.

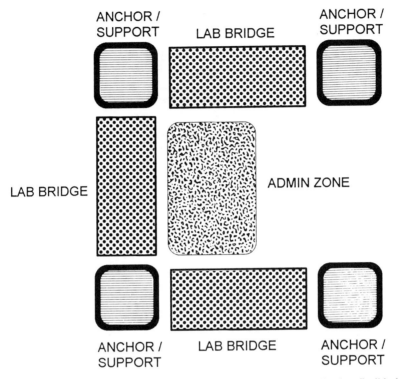

FIGURE 7. Anchor and bridge plan arrangement. Flexibility scenario allowing flexible lab zones to span between fixed support zones.

A potential consequence of this scenario is illustrated in FIGURE 4 where the lab building has grown an office building exterior with the lab space sandwiched in the middle.

Lab Equipment Is Replacing Lab Furniture

The traditional lab bench, whose purpose has always been to provide a work surface and to distribute electrical and piped utilities in the lab, is being displaced by equipment that comes with its own storage unit and work surface. Furthermore, it is portable.

New Utility Distribution Patterns in the Lab

Sophisticated instrumentation requires so many different connections for piped services, specialty gases, electrical power, and computer tie-ins to local

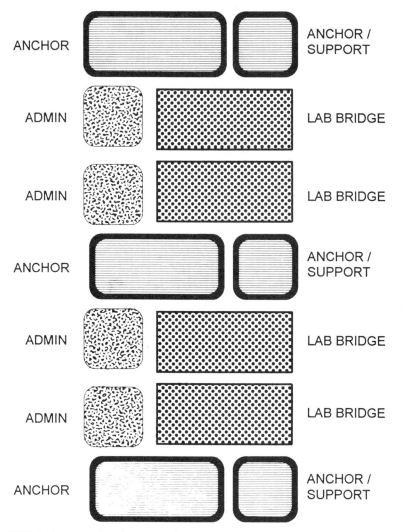

FIGURE 8. Anchor and bridge—vertical arrangement. Flexibility scenario adapting anchor and bridge to a vertical scheme. Individual floors would be dedicated to labs or support.

data networks that access from all sides is frequently required. Access to the rear or side of the equipment is also necessary for calibration of equipment. The traditional lab bench, which only allows access from the front, is becoming an obstruction for certain types of instrumentation. An effective option for instrumentation laden labs is split benches (FIG. 5), which provides a service aisle between two benches with services running along the backs of benches. Another alternate delivery strategy is to group piped services verti-

FIGURE 9. Shell labs—raw unoccupied version.

cally, which acknowledges that equipment can be stacked and takes advantage of the lab's vertical as well as horizontal dimensions (FIG. 6).

Options for Flexibility

The need for facility flexibility to accommodate change in lab utilization, layout, staffing, and group organization will be a basic requirement of research facility design rather than an option. Currently, there are many approaches to achieving flexibility: flexible furniture, moveable walls, modular or generic

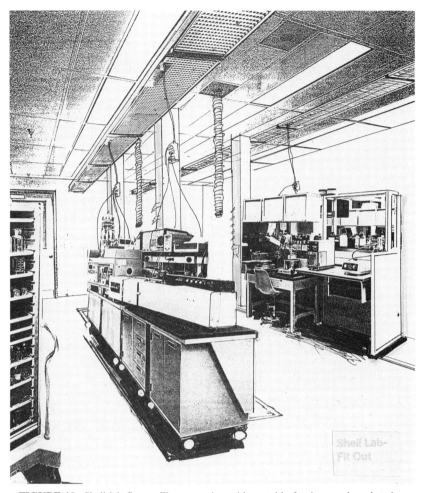

FIGURE 10. Shell lab fit-out. Fit-out version with portable furniture and workstation.

labs, open field planning, interstitial floors, which removes service distribution as a fixed element from the floor plan. But, for the purpose of this discussion, I offer three alternative scenarios:

- Anchor and Bridge—Consider open areas of flexible, utility rich undifferentiated lab space as bridges spanning nodes or concentrations of fixed, distinct, and specialized support spaces (anchors) containing functions such as tissue culture, environmental rooms, chromatography, NMRs, EMs, mass specs, glass wash, media prep, etc. Office space,

FIGURE 11. Plug-in adaptability. Microenvironment lab module in trailer being plugged into a research facility.

FIGURE 12. Sensitivity to risk. Wearing your protective environment.

FIGURE 13. Ph.D/MTV. The postwar baby boomers reach scientific and managerial maturity.

FIGURE 14. Break room as game room. Using facilities to restore the spirit of play back into science.

another large block of undifferentiated space capable of reallocation, would be adjacent to but separate from the lab blocks. The diagrams illustrate a plan arrangement (FIG. 7) and a vertically stacked configuration (FIG. 8). These arrangements also lend themselves to circulation patterns that separate staff from service and material flow if such separations are desired.

FIGURE 15. R&D facilities as real estate commodities.

FIGURE 16. Benign buildings. Can you clean out the ductwork?

- The Lab as a Shell—In this version, the lab is a raw, utility rich, but otherwise bare space (FIG. 9). Piped services are delivered via service columns, electrical and computer services run in overhead cable trays, local exhaust drops in the form of elephant trunks or snorkels are strategically located over the benchable area, lighting and sprinkler lines run in the ceiling above (the ceiling itself is optional). A zone for benching and equipment is indicated. This room is capable of accommodating many different layout alternatives, which can either be built-in, rolled in, or plugged in very quickly. One is shown in FIGURE 10.

FIGURE 17. Existing lab building.

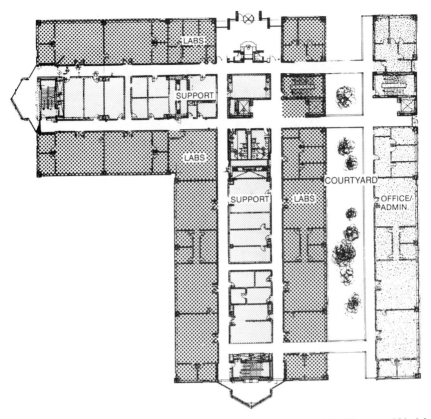

FIGURE 18. Office papoose—plan of lab block with office wing added. All space within lab building is now labs and support space. Lab offices and team work space is now in a separate building block.

- The Specialty Plug-In Lab—Finally, an extreme view of plug-in adaptability. Labs are now fabricated in transportable trailers 8 feet wide and 40 feet long. Specialty labs (see the variety under the description of Anchors and Bridges) or general purpose labs as microenvironments could be transported and plugged into a facility both architecturally and mechanically as illustrated in FIGURE 11.

Connectivity

The scientific enterprise is global. It is too broad in scope and moving too rapidly in all directions for any one individual or institution to operate in isolation. Connectivity via information networks is a prerequisite. This

FIGURE 19. Lab building with office papoose—model version.

FIGURE 20. Deep dish R&D. Satellite dishes as the new lab building appurtenance.

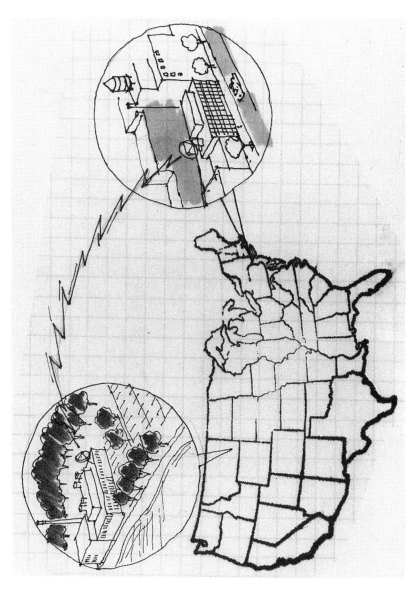

FIGURE 21. Cross talk. Communications and operational control between far-flung research facilities via telecommunications systems.

FIGURE 22. Environmentally designed facilities. Sooner or later lab buildings will be required to develop their own ameliorative biosphere.

FIGURE 23. Return of the R&D facility to the city.

FIGURE 24. High-tech image. Virtual reality helmet.

FIGURE 25. Low-tech image. Street-person functioning as a recycler.

requirement is likely to have two major facility consequences on the labs of the future:

- Telecommunications capability of voice, signal, and real time data will become an essential, major, and visible building system. The more bandwidth the better. More on this in "Part II."

- Libraries in research facilities will become an essential connection point between the individual facility and the scientific, legal, regulatory, and market community it is a part of. There will always be paper in the form of journals references and monographs, but computer and information systems will become the dominant technology giving the library its information storage capacity and its connectivity. Research facilities will need libraries in some form or will need ready access to one. Access will be both physical, for social reasons, and via telecommunications systems for connections to journals, data bases, information scientists. Irrespective of size, libraries will require good data systems and dedicated staffs to operate properly.

The Increasing Sensitivity to Risk and Hazard

The ability to detect and define risk is growing. So is our sensitivity to it. In turn, this will increase the demands on the facility to shield, protect, mitigate, or eliminate risks and hazards. Anticipate more containment of both known and potentially hazardous processes. Consider that there will be increased, even extreme forms of personal protection such as the suit where you wear your protective environment (FIG. 12). And be prepared for the discontinuities in utilization and behavior that will emerge from the conflict between the regimented practices required to cope with risk and the desire for free and easy access that is fundamental to the scientific spirit.

Demography Is Changing

The demography of the scientific community is changing, and it is changing everything along with it. Today's scientists are the products of the postwar baby boom. They are younger and grew up professionally in an environment where they expect more certainty of performance (i.e., quality), more comfort and user friendliness, and more concessions to their lifestyle from the work environment, especially since there are fewer distinctions made between work and life, than the preceding generation of post-WWII scientists. They want quality, convenience, and fun (FIG. 13).

The competition to attract and retain quality scientific talent will increase. This is a hard group to please. In addition to all of their basic scientific needs (labs, offices, support space, equipment), the facility must also provide those elements that support organizational life–break or interaction areas, seminar and conference spaces, video conferencing, and the amenities of daily life (ATMs, round-the-clock food services, videotape rental libraries, dry cleaning services, recreational facilities for both health and play). Erasing the demarcation of work life and the other activities of daily living will be a major facility asset. Scientists work all the time and value their time highly. That is why these amenities will become so important. The fewer obstacles to spending time at work the better. They also like to play. Play is intermingled with work and is a basic strategy in the pursuit of science both in conceptualization as well as experimentation.

So let us reevaluate the break or interaction area. Out with the space reserved for quiet contemplation and in with the multipurpose game rooms (Fig. 14)!

Research and Development Facilities as Real Estate Commodities

The increasing movement toward consolidation within the pharmaceutical, electronics, chemical, and consumer products industries is forcing us to consider research facilities as real estate commodities (Fig. 15). They are built, then they are traded with greater frequency. Prudence dictates that consideration be given to future reuse possibilities both for other R&D as well as non-R&D organizations and functions. The den will have implications on the design and configuration of the facility (e.g., the floor plan must be sized for both lab and for office occupancies; it should be capable of multitenancy). This trend will also require that for retenancy, systems can be cleaned and be certified as benign (Fig. 16).

AN ARCHITECT'S VIEWPOINT: PART II

Increasing the Amount of Office Space

The pressures driving the need for more office space and the migration of that space to the perimeter of the floor plan were discussed earlier. One possibility might be that offices are divorced from the labs entirely and are housed in a separate connected building block adjacent to a lab wing, which is completely occupied by lab and research support space. The office block would be, in effect, a "papoose." Figures 17, 18, and 19 compare a basic lab building with its "papoose" version in both plan and model.

Communications Technologies

Telecommunications will become a dominant technology, and lab buildings will sprout satellite dishes the way they currently exhibit exhaust stacks (FIG. 20). The dish will become the new appurtenance. Whether they can be integrated as a conscious design element or will be relegated to being a kind of stigma (as smoke stacks were during the Industrial Revolution) is not certain.

Another and perhaps more profound effect of telecommunications and control technologies might enable widely separated research facilities to be so closely linked that they can operate as a unified institution, one part operating as the head, the other as the body or the instrument (FIG. 21). This could have wide applicability for collaboration and joint work on a common problem, for connecting far-flung physical and intellectual resources, even for operating hazardous functions remotely from other elements of the research facility.

The Pressure for the Environmentally Benign Facility

The public's concerns with risks of research, their fear of technology, and the demand for absolute accountability for each potential risk will impose upon research facilities the demand that, environmentally, they be risk free. Research facilities might be held to a standard that all research related elements and wastes emerge significantly purer, cleaner then the normal or domestic waste streams. Lab buildings will need to develop, maintain, and manage not just engineered systems, but their own micro climates to achieve such a standard (FIG. 22).

The Hostility of the Suburbs and the Return to the City

For over 50 years, research facilities have been migrating to the suburbs where land and energy were inexpensive. This trend may be abating in the face of increased suburban hostility to overdevelopment generally, and to the perceived risks imposed by research facilities specifically.

One possibility is that research facilities may move further out to exurban locations as suggested by FIGURE 21. Another possibility may be the return to the city, to the industrial areas close to the urban core, which have been vacated by manufacturing industries (FIG. 23). There is a desire that is particularly strong among the younger, more entrepreneurial scientists, to be close to the heart of the cities where the financial, intellectual, marketing, legal, and creative capital, and a broad array of services, are all located.

A Final Word on Technology and Creativity

I have one final speculation. It is about the sources of creativity. The virtual reality helmet (FIG. 24) is our image of the innovative, the technologically sophisticated, the creative. Indeed, it is technically sweet and of the moment. FIGURE 25 is a sketch I did of a street person I spotted one day, someone who, with no resources, invented himself as a recycling entrepreneur. As architects and engineers, we deliver technological solutions to a multifacted need–scientific, organizational, economic, regulatory, sociological. We never know where the best insights or technology will come from. The street person created a wildly imaginative and appropriate mobile sorting vehicle out of a supermarket shopping cart, milk crates, wire, reflectors, and rearview mirrors. It is a reminder that we live in a sea of creativity. The possibilities are endless. We just need to open our minds wide enough to perceive it.

And so it is with thinking about the future.

Speculating About the Laboratory of the Future

Space and Circulation Concepts

JEFFREY S. FRENCH

Ballinger
One Commerce Square
2005 Market Street
Suite 1500
Philadelphia, Pennsylvania 19103-7088

Of the many planning decisions in research facility design, few are more fundamental than the overall circulation concept and, specifically, the relationship of laboratory to office space and to lab support space. Numerous planning models are being tested and refined, suggesting that some research organizations prioritize accessibility to shared equipment from the lab, others favor the more remote ''core space'' concept, and still others prefer the flexibility inherent in schemes in which lab support is virtually indistinguishable from lab modules. In all cases, issues such as daylight/environment and safety continue to grow in importance. Each new research facility is, in some way, anticipating the future, hoping that today's judgments will prove viable in the years ahead.

As we look to the future, we must consider how emerging influences, some of which have clearly begun to reveal themselves, might reshape the lab/office/lab support configuration. Despite the differences in the research facility needs of one scientific discipline vs. another, or of a corporation vs. an academic medical center, some concerns remain relatively universal. Through an examination of several recent research facility examples, one can begin to understand the trends as today's planners perceive them, and how a vision of the future is manifested in their architectural layout ideas.

THE MODULAR PLAN

''Modular planning,'' the repetition of identical space dimensions and proportions, or increments thereof, has been the foundation of laboratory flexibility for many years; it will likely remain as such for the foreseeable future. At Indiana University's School of Medicine in Indianapolis, a medical research building was completed in 1989 utilizing a 10-foot planning increment, with a 20-foot depth on one side of the single corridor and a 25-foot

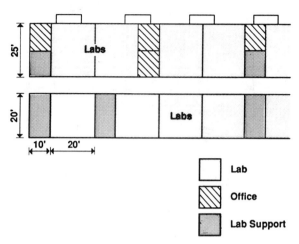

FIGURE 1. Indiana University School of Medicine Medical Science Research Building. Architect: Ellerbe Becket.

depth on the other (FIG. 1). The typical laboratory is a double module, or 20 feet wide. In this instance, the modular approach allows a 10-foot-wide office or lab support zone to be integrated into this perimeter lab area at virtually any point between the labs themselves. Lab support elements include such spaces as controlled temperature (hot or cold) rooms, darkrooms, lab equipment rooms, tissue culture rooms, glasswash rooms, or simply storage areas for samples, glassware, incoming or outgoing materials.

While the modular plan is designed to anticipate potential changes in the ratios of space types, a number of concerns have been expressed by the laboratory occupants. First, one must frequently exit or enter an office only through a lab, an area of higher hazard. This safety dilemma is particularly acute when bringing visitors into these offices. Second, senior investigator offices occur on only one side of the corridor, causing a degree of remoteness from labs that is not particularly popular. Nevertheless, the modular nature of the plan and the corresponding flexibility in air-handling systems and utilities have provided a vehicle for change as the evolving research mission redefines facility needs.

The University of Alabama at Birmingham (UAB) has recently opened its new biomedical research facility. Like Indiana University, UAB utilizes a single corridor, attempting to maximize building efficiency (the amount of assignable area as a percentage of total building area; assignable area does not include corridors, mechanical equipment rooms, stairs, elevators, toilet rooms, and similar nonfunctional components). However, UAB has internal-

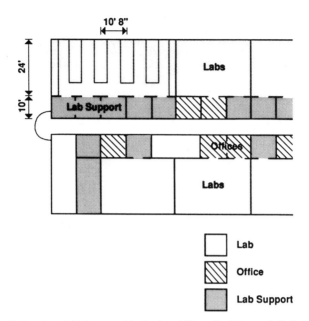

FIGURE 2. University of Alabama at Birmingham Biomedical Research Building. Architect: the Ritchie Organization.

ized lab support and office spaces along the corridor, while the labs occupy the perimeter (FIG. 2). Consequently, safety is enhanced in terms of accessibility to offices. Labs may be any combination of open, multiple-module configurations, or enclosed single-module areas. This type of flexibility represents an attempt to recognize potential volatility in the grant-driven research environment. As research teams and projects change, the facility may change as well. As we will see in some other organizations' experiences, however, the type of change most frequently occurring today affects lab support space rather than labs themselves. It is unclear whether the UAB diagram will be forgiving in its accommodation of significant increases in lab support requirements.

INCREASING LAB SUPPORT NEEDS

The extraordinary evolution in equipment technology has spawned an ever-increasing need for lab support space to house it. Although the size of individual pieces of equipment continues to decrease, the total amount of sophisticated computer-based lab monitoring equipment does not. A trend that may have among the most significant effects on future research facility planning is, indeed, the increasing percentage of shared equipment or lab

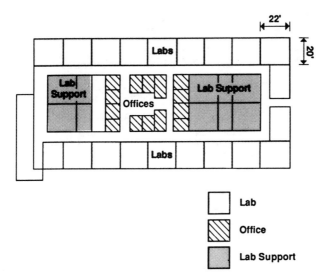

FIGURE 3. The Bowman Gray School of Medicine of Wake Forest University Hanes Research Tower. Architect: Henningson Durham Richardson.

support space relative to total research area. In the many facilities that are ill-equipped to adapt to this trend, the deficiencies are readily apparent. Lab benches have become "shelves" for the equipment, rather than actual work areas.

At Wake Forest University's Bowman Gray School of Medicine in Winston-Salem, North Carolina, the Hanes Research Tower was designed to anticipate the emergence of lab support space as a major space determinant. Rather than integrate lab support into the perimeter lab zone, as in the Indiana University or UAB examples, a central support core was created (FIG. 3). The concept of a central support core, surrounded by a "racetrack" corridor and perimeter labs and offices, can probably be described as the current state of the art. Some version of the two-corridor, or racetrack, scheme can be found on countless academic and corporate campuses.

At Bowman Gray's Hanes Tower, the centralized core is unusually deep, nearly twice the depth of the rather shallow 20-foot perimeter lab zone. Such a dimension would readily accommodate a lab to lab support ratio of nearly one to one. Unfortunately, the clarity of the concept was compromised by the insertion of a large cluster of faculty offices in the center of the core. While this concept does foster a certain amount of the interaction it was intended to encourage, a windowless and unpleasant "faculty ghetto" has resulted. The building also has a very low floor-to-floor height dimension

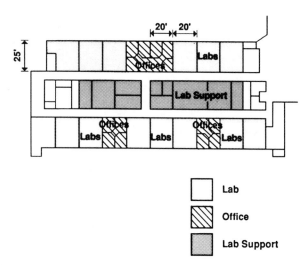

FIGURE 4. The Bowman Gray School of Medicine of Wake Forest University Nutrition Research Center. Architect: Ballinger.

(for a research facility) of eleven feet. As a result, the air distribution system is so difficult to revise that it effectively eliminates any ability to convert this office zone into the more air-intensive lab or lab support space. The net effect of all this is an inflexible building whose original concept had promised adaptability to increasing equipment space demands.

In a subsequent plan for the new Center for Research on Human Nutrition and Chronic Disease Prevention (know simply as the Nutrition Research Center, or NRC), Bowman Gray has once again adopted a racetrack scheme with a centralized lab support core (FIG. 4). In this facility, however, the modular core dimensions are identical to those of the lab zone. Thus, the spaces are interchangeable. Offices occupy only the perimeter modules, either grouped around a secretary in clusters of six offices each, or into single modules of three offices each. As a result, daylight reaches labs and offices alike, internalizing only support space; noisy equipment is removed from both labs and office areas; comparable benefits in safety and interaction are achieved; and the appropriate (today) two-to-one ratio of lab to lab support space is provided while enabling that ratio to change over time.

In their new Medical Research Center in Philadelphia, Pennsylvania, the Lankenau Hospital blended the concept of an integrated lab/office/lab support perimeter zone (not unlike Indiana University and UAB) with the central support core idea (similar to Bowman Gray's NRC). In the 30-foot-deep perimeter zone, module widths vary from 22 to 24 feet, with the narrower

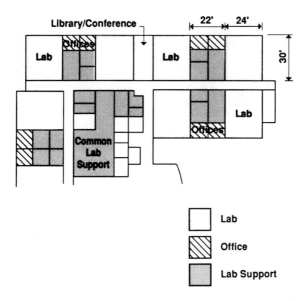

FIGURE 5. The Lankenau Hospital Medical Research Center. Architect: Ewing Cole Cherry Parsky.

module consisting of two 11-foot-wide perimeter offices. The internalized area of the module is dedicated support space for the adjoining lab (FIG. 5). Sometimes this space is open to the lab, and sometimes it is closed off, but it is always occupied by freezers, incubators, biological safety cabinets, or simply storage. In addition, the scheme offers the central core for common lab support such as controlled temperature rooms, tissue culture lab, darkroom, and large glasswash room.

With some support space adjacent and some more remote from the lab, the Lankenau concept recognizes the differences between frequent and occasional usage of support equipment. The ratio of lab to lab support space here is nearly three to two, yet with the building only one year old, lab support space is rapidly becoming inadequate. In its first year, the facility has housed only half of the senior investigators ultimately expected, yet the lab support areas are nearly at capacity. In fact, the area designated in FIGURE 5 as "Library/Conference" is now wired for shared lab equipment along one wall.

A very different approach to the accommodation of shared lab support equipment has been taken at such locations as the University of Miami, Johns Hopkins University, and SmithKline Beecham's Research and Development Consolidation facility in Swedeland, Pennsylvania. Recognizing the tendency

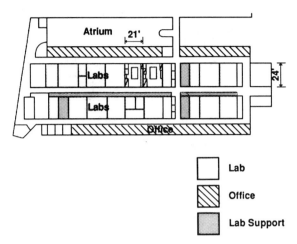

FIGURE 6. SmithKline Beecham Corporation R&D Consolidation: Molecular Biology. Architect: Ballinger.

to allow equipment to "spill over" into corridors when alternative space is unavailable, SmithKline Beecham chose to plan for this, rather than to allow it to happen randomly. By utilizing a central service corridor, and by programming it to accommodate specific pieces of scientific equipment, SmithKline Beecham could reduce the number of lab modules devoted to equipment or support space (FIG. 6).

To further understand the increasing demand for lab support space, one may consider the experience of the University of Michigan Medical School in Ann Arbor, Michigan. In their Medical Sciences Research Building Number One (MSRB-I), Michigan utilized a central support core surrounded by a racetrack corridor, similar to Bowman Gray's NRC but in a triangular configuration (FIG. 7). In that building, completed in 1986, the central core was very small. Separated by "public" corridors on all three sides, the scheme offered a lab to support ratio of approximately five to one. Not surprisingly, the lab support space proved to be inadequate. Thus, on the later MSRB-III, scheduled for completion in 1994 (FIG. 8), several significant changes have occurred while the basic triangular concept remains. To begin with, the central core contains much more space; the building is bulkier than MSRB-I, and all of the increased area is in lab support space. Secondly, open labs with "ghost" corridors (implied corridors running between a wall and the ends of lab benches) now appear on two sides in lieu of the public corridors, returning space to the labs. Finally, lab support alcoves have been located within the labs, at the perimeter of the central core, providing flexible space for dedicated support equipment, tissue culture operations, or computer space. The resultant lab to support space ratio is nearly two-to-one.

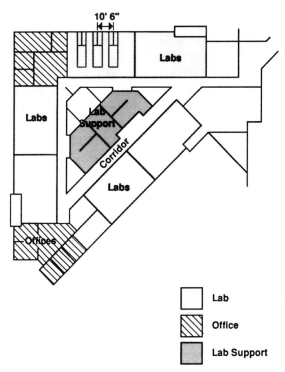

10' 6"

Labs

Labs

Lab Support

Corridor

Labs

Offices

☐ Lab

▨ Office

▨ Lab Support

FIGURE 7. University of Michigan Medical School Medical Sciences Research Building I. Architect: Jickling Lyman Powell.

ADDITIONAL TRENDS AND TOMORROW'S RESPONSE

There would appear to be little doubt that a dominant trend in research facility planning is the allocation of ever-increasing space for laboratory support and equipment. A two-to-one ratio of lab to lab support is common, particularly in the biological research disciplines, and a one-to-one ratio is on the way. The ability of a facility to "flex" between labs and support space will likely be the basis of sound, modular planning in the years ahead. The number of computer-based laboratory monitoring units will continue to rise, more than offsetting the continued size reduction in the individual components. Much of this equipment will be floor mounted, or, at the very least, unlikely to fit comfortably on a traditional 30-inch-deep lab benchtop.

Wider lab modules have been emerging with a 22-foot "typical lab" replacing the 20-foot version. However, in virtually all existing examples known to this author, the extra space afforded by the larger dimension is in

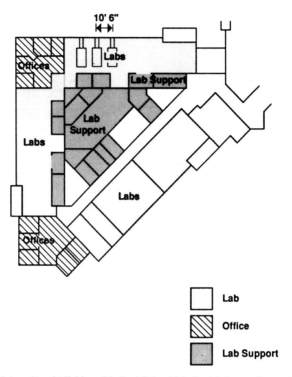

FIGURE 8. University of Michigan Medical School Medical Sciences Research Building III. Architect: Jickling Lyman Powell.

the aisle space between the benches, not in the benches themselves. Given the extraordinary amount of equipment that now occupies these lab benches, particularly in analytical settings, it might seem appropriate to consider a deeper typical benchtop throughout. Much of the equipment is too deep for the countertop of today's lab; this is exacerbated by the presence of lab service outlets (air, gas, vacuum, etc.) on many benches. On the other hand, continued miniaturization may eliminate the need for extra space in either the bench depth or the aisle.

Some research organizations are already beginning to abandon the traditional "square feet per person" method of allocating space to senior scientists. This is due, in part, to the same trend. With equipment occupying, or even replacing, the lab benches to such a large extent in a traditional lab layout (two wall benches and a center island), the total square foot area becomes a rather meaningless measure. UAB has developed an approach to space allocation based on linear feet of bench per person, in an effort to find a more appropriate tool. The dilemma here may be the extent to which an institution's culture, based for so long on square feet of space, will easily adapt to an allocation model that reduces it in the name of efficiency. If senior researchers, who have lived in the "space is power" era, perceive any new allocation model as a disguise for space reduction, then the model will fail.

Safety concerns, and evolving regulations to address them, are destined to have potentially profound impacts on research facility planning in the future. One result will be the continued separation of office space from traditional laboratory functions. One might speculate that office sizes will decrease; with the elimination of paper in this electronic age, file cabinets become unnecessary, along with the space required to house them. In any case, very few labs are likely to be planned, in the next decade, that do not remove senior scientist and technician office workstations from the immediate lab environment. This evolution will not be easy. Some concede that too extensive a separation may yield less-effective science, that "touch, feel, and smell" remain essential to scientific advancement. In fact, a hierarchy is implied in some research facilities in which the occupants of semiremote, enclosed offices are perceived as "above" the hands-on lab work. Also conspiring to keep these functions intermingled is the feeling among many scientists that tomorrow's dramatic breakthroughs will occur in the boundaries or at the edges of individual research disciplines, rather than in traditional modes of thinking and working. Nevertheless, issues of liability and exposure, industrial hygiene, and waste disposal all are suggesting that scientific personnel should not be exposed to experiments unnecessarily.

Perhaps one may challenge the prevalent culture in the United States, which offers a dedicated and personalized office or workstation to all building occupants. With the extensive collaboration and interaction between research organizations, one rarely sees all occupants of a lab in the area at the same time. Might duplication be reduced by depersonalizing office areas and providing only enough space that a percentage of the total users can be accommodated at any one time? One could imagine an organization of 300 employees having a bank of workstation "units" which can be dislodged from the "storage" area, wheeled to a spot on the floor where it can be "plugged in" to data and electrical power, and replaced at the end of the day. Only enough units, and the corresponding space, are provided to house 200 at a time, since no more than that are ever in the facility at one time. Some people may work at home, linked electronically to the rest of the research community and relevant data bases. This would further reduce the space requirements of a given facility.

One safety-related trend may actually begin to reverse itself. In recent years, virtually all wet chemistry/synthesis-type work has been conducted inside fume hoods, rather than on lab benches, affording safe evacuation of potentially hazardous fumes and gases. This has led to a dramatic increase in the amount of fume hood space required, often at the expense of nonexhausted bench area. However, restrictions on sizes and volumes of material permitted in laboratory environments may yield more and more microscale/ milligram-level work than in the past. There may be less waste, less hazard, and, thus, less fume hood requirements.

As the financial pressure to do more with less continues, and it surely will, increased sharing and duplication avoidance will result. Equipment will be scheduled for greater utilization, perhaps even with outside agents (e.g., university-industry partnerships); the extensive sharing, and the isolation of office and computer or data entry stations from the lab environment, may result in still greater amounts of space allocated for lab support functions.

While some of the ideas put forth in these pages are purely speculative, one observation seems particularly appropriate. The traditional wall bench/ island/wall bench layout of a lab has existed for nearly a century. It seems an extraordinary coincidence that this model has remained virtually intact despite the incredible advancements in science and research technology over that period. Can this laboratory configuration really be the single most effective means of accommodating today's sophisticated, technology-enhanced research, just as it was decades ago, prior to the arrival of such technology and equipment?

Perhaps the most logical approach to research facility planning is one that does not attempt to accurately predict the future. Rather, strategy must be developed to accommodate multiple scenarios, measured in terms of uncertainty and impact. The optimum laboratory is one that can adapt to the broadest array of possibilities, one that can respond to events most likely to occur and with the greatest potential impact, and one that not only adjusts to advancements in technology, but encourages them.

Some Speculations About the Lab of the Future

An Engineer's Viewpoint

TIMOTHY D. BAKER

R. G. Vanderweil Engineers, Inc.
266 Summer Street
Boston, Massachusetts 02210-1112

Engineers have a special part to play in the development of what will surely be the future for research and development facilities construction and operation. Because of our responsibilities to our profession as described by the requirements of our registration as PEs, professional engineers, we are bound legally by our "standard of care" and by statutes including the statutes of liability for our work. Engineers today are predisposed to support, in fact, to lead the march to the future.

In the early 1970s, when lines of empty tanked automobiles were all over the headlines, all waiting for a fraction of a "fill up," it all of a sudden became politically acceptable and correct to conserve energy. Energy conservation was thrust on the American people by the politics of the times, and the MEP engineering community responded.

New and expanded industries were formed to find and produce new and better building materials and insulations. Replacements for asbestos were sought. New products and services like thermography, glazing and shading, high-efficiency motors, standards for EERs for refrigerators in the home, and even government-mandated reduced energy consumption for residential and commercial buildings were all fostered.

Looking back, it seemed that as quickly as the energy crisis came, it also went. The engineering and technical advances however remain. There remain today natural energy conservation guidelines for buildings by which all facility design engineers must abide. It is a wonder where these "savings" in energy went and to whose benefit the conservation efforts accrued, since today we are as dependent on foreign oil energy as we were in 1973 or worse.

The lab of the future should anticipate the probable curtailments in the use of air, water, and power that must surely occur over the next two to three decades. Engineers, especially those of us that are in professions that deal directly with the design, management, and distribution of energy within buildings, including that spent for the environment within the buildings themselves, should be anticipating the potential for less available clean air, water and electrical energy that will arrive as we face the oncoming ecological crisis in our world. Our leadership in the next few decades must occur voluntarily or, believe it or not, we will again be relegated to a reactive response to again mostly politically driven untrained crisis policy management.

Because the lab of today is such an energy and operationally intensive structure, coupled with its traditional reputation for reduced levels of building efficiency, it seems that these two issues must be resolved immediately. Further, we must reduce the overall use of water and the resulting consequent need for energy intensive wastewater treatment. Third, we must reduce the use of electrical energy in buildings so that there will remain sufficient energy for other uses. Three speculations in order of air, water, and electrical power are presented hereinafter.

Air

For content, a paragraph from Vice President Al Gore's work *Earth in the Balance* from page 84: "The relatively small number of air molecules in the atmosphere have been continuously recycled through animals and plants since oxygen was first produced in large volume by photosynthetic microorganisms almost 3 billion years ago. Those animals and plants adapted over long periods, to the precise combination of molecules that have been present in the air throughout most of evolution. . . . In every breath we take, we bathe our lungs in a homogeneous sample of that same air–many trillions of molecules of it–with at least a few in each breath that were also breathed by Buddha at some point during his life, and a like number that were breathed by Jesus, Moses, Mohammed–as well as Hitler, Stalin and Genghis Khan."

It was only 10 years or so ago that engineers discovered that chlorofluorocarbons (CFC's) were contributing to the thinning of the ozone layer. The "ozone hole" now above Antarctica "covers an area three times as big as the contiguous United States."

We can only speculate today on what other chemical effluent that we are now releasing will affect what part of our fragile world next. For this reason, researchers in R&D facilities and the design community responsible for the actual design of these facilities must realize, or be made to realize, that our atmosphere can no longer be considered a universal dumping ground.

Within an R&D facility, safe science must continue to be done within regulated atmospheres, but engineers must find a way to spend less and use less energy capital in the form of reduced air usage in each lab. Fume hood use will, in the future, be tightly regulated. A "hood in each module" will no longer be the norm, giving way to an "air guzzler tax" not unlike the "gas guzzler tax" on large volume engines in automobiles.

We know today how to reduce the air flow through a fume hood without reducing the level of safety for the scientist, but we also are aware of the pained reluctance of the investigators to be relegated to some perception of reduced level of fume hood usage. There are today, on the market and in use, shielded fume hoods incorporating both horizontal and vertical sash operations that cut flow through air use in hoods to less than half. Ironically, this approach is not enforced in our country most likely because it requires the PIs (principal investigators) to learn a new way of physical operation at their workplace.

Today there are only two fume hood manufacturers who have been approved by certified testing for hoods that can be used by the United States Environmental Protection Agency (EPA). Both of these hoods are full open sash, 1400 CFM 6-foot hoods. At the same time, for profit, R&D workplaces are being fitted with 6-foot hoods that use only 700 CFM, their use promulgated by bottom line considerations. The lab of the future will surely incorporate the new design hood or they will be "taxed" for their air use.

The ductwork and piping systems we design must conserve space within the building. We must take advantage of our present day capabilities such as low temperature air and expanded temperature differentials for the air and water streams.

As the total air use in the lab is reduced because of more efficient low air hood designs, engineers will save the energy associated with supplying and exhausting the lab air.

In some applications, supply air for comfort conditioning in the lab could be provided from low-temperature apparatus. In today's lab, supply air at approximately 55°F is needed to maintain the lab at 72° to 75°F. This allows a ductwork air transport temperature of roughly 20°F or less. A low-temperature design would supply air at 42° to 48°F for an effective air temperature differential of say 28°F. Since air *quantity* is directly proportional to the effective temperature differential, the same BTUs would be capable of being carried in a reduced size duct at a ratio of size corresponding to the ratio of the temperature differentials. For our example, the duct cross section could theoretically be reduced by $(1-20°/28°) = 28.5\%$.

There is not an architect in this country that wouldn't applaud a 28% decrease in the amount of ductwork space required for these facilities.

In the future, this technique could be applied but must be coupled with additional investigation of the cost/benefits of producing this low-temperature air and the reheat (which will have to be done with recovered heat energy) from the refrigerant system.

Modern laboratories today incorporate a "built-in" amount of office space within the lab for charting, data transmission, storage, and analysis. Most R&D facilities actually have office components within. This combination space is very convenient for the researcher but leads to making the lab side less efficient and the office side very energy intensive.

We knowingly provide such combination spaces for the PI's convenience. One of the most critical design criteria today in lab planning is "how far do I have to walk to get from my office to my lab?" Signs of change are coming. NIH, the National Institutes of Health, about five years ago began to mandate that instead of continuing the policy where long-term use of nonhuman primates occurred in the PI's space (requiring transport of the primate to the lab), the primates would stay within the primate facility and the researcher would do the moving. Many facilities are starting to look at keeping the office activities out of the lab; this is certainly a trend of the future.

Moving the air within the R&D facility consumes 90% of the ventilation energy budget within a building. Some years ago, ASHRAE, the American Society of Heating Refrigeration and Air Conditioning Engineers, described an "air transport factor" for air handling systems. This factor became part of the energy conservation guidelines promulgated by ASHRAE and essentially limited air provided to a fixed ratio of delivered to fan horsepower such that ductwork and equipment would tend to be closer to the area served. The future R&D facilities will see these ratios come down and, with them, the level of motor horsepower use in the lab will correspondingly be reduced and the air side systems equipment will have to be located closer and closer to their point of use.

Finally, there is the possibility of energy credits against construction: this is both a building issue and an energy conservation issue. Here in New York City two months ago, a reconstruction project was noted for its energy conservation approach. Of note to their credit was the energy conservation that accrued to their project because of the tons of steel and concrete that did *not* need to be created since they reconfigured, i.e., reused an existing structure.

The speculation for the lab of the future must include the readaptation of the buildings of the past. Such an approach would be politically attractive as more inner city presently unused properties would be put back onto the tax roles. We are currently working on an adaptive reuse of an abandoned warehouse in downtown Boston, Massachusetts. This 1,000,000 sf project already contains 150,000 tons of concrete, steel, rebar, and limestone and granite that will not have to be remanufactured. We speculate that lab facility managers will more and more look to the reuse of such facilities as a way to "cost avoid" the basic construction processes that are involved with new structures. Further, tax laws and incentives will be arranged to provide financial incentives to lab R&D owners to locate and relocate to these available sites.

Water

Again from Vice President Al Gore's book *Earth In The Balance* page 100: "We depend on fresh water which is only 2.5 percent of the total amount of water on earth. Most of that is locked away as ice in Antarctica and to a lesser extent in Greenland. Groundwater makes up most of what remains, leaving less than .01 percent for all the lakes, creeks, rivers and rainfall."

As an example of the problem, from page 111. Egypt, whose 55 millon people rely almost exclusively on the Nile for drinking water will have, by conservative estimates, a population of at least 100 million people within 35 years. Yet the Nile will still have no more water than it did when Moses was found in the bulrushes—in fact, it will have less, because Ethiopia and Sudan are upstream and have even faster rates of population growth.

As engineers, we see restrictions on water use and effluent discharge every day. The lab of the future should be planning for ways to minimize water use now as well as seeking ways to approach "almost" zero net effluent discharge.

At the EPA facility currently under design, we have already proposed and have been directed to proceed with some interesting water-management techniques.

1. Gray water reuse. In Research Triangle Park, it is economically attractive for EPA to collect clear water wastes from drinking fountains and hand wash sinks, to store it, and recycle it to the flush valve fixtures within the building.
2. Dehumidification—clear water. We use so much air at EPA and the outdoor air contains so much moisture (Raleigh, North Carolina) that we are projecting, via the cooling coil dehumidification process, that we can conservatively reclaim nearly 25 gallons per minute that is clear, clean, and available for additional reuse. This will amount to nearly 750,000 gallons annually. When not reused in the gray water recycling system, it will be possible to use this clear effluent for dilution in the interior waste treatment system and on the landscape as a source of irrigation.
3. Cooling tower make-up. Traditionally, cooling towers, by adiabatic saturation, cool condenser water by fan forced heat rejection to the atmosphere. In the process, traditional towers in this size class lose 1.5% of total water volume to evaporation and another .5% to what we call "blowdown." Blowdown essentially wastes water where particulate concentrations have built up that could materially damage the cooling equipment.

The towers we are using at EPA include centrifugal solids separators that, with tangential velocity, separate the particulates and recycle the cleaned water. The system savings at full load amount to as much as 45 gallons per minute for a potential savings each summer of 6.5 million gallons of water. The actual amount is enormous because of the size of the system and the fact that labs and their cooling systems, including the cooling towers, operate 24 hours a day.

Waste Discharge

As municipal water treatment facilities continue to be overtaxed, the restrictions that will be applied to R&D facilities operators will increase. Presently we screen for temperature and pH; in the future, heavy metal reclaim could be imposed. Already today in plating operations, we are recovering the precious metals. The labs of the future could be required to reclaim the mercury, lead, and other metals that we currently pass along. Such reclamation will be good for the processors and for the environment.

Electrical Power

Electrical utilities' demands for power have, on a national basis, not increased as quickly as was projected in the 1960s and 1970s. But, regionally not much additional generating capacity is being added. Present capacity provided by nuclear power is aging and more plants are being shut down than are new plants being proposed. As a minimum, if the planning for new nuclear capacity began today, the first megawatt of anticipated power would be more than 15 years away.

Speculation on electricity use in the lab is that electricity use could potentially move to zero net increase over 1993 levels. This speculation is based on the idea that labs are becoming more and more automated and electronically driven and that the energy use on modern technological data gathering is actually decreasing. Microelectronics is making a significant "flattening" of the growth curve of energy usage in the R&D setting. As the energy usage in the lab pod flattens, and as the make-up air load based on reduced sizes of hoods comes into play, the total environmental load impact of these facilities will start to show a net decrease.

Lastly the R&D electrical system in new facilities will be capable of self-regulation. As engineers, we are presently pushing what we have described as the "concept of the unoccupied lab." Simply put, the best way to conserve energy is to turn off the energy-consuming facilities. The unoccupied lab concept is this, that—rather than consider the in lab facilities to be always on and to then effect conservation—we provide a lab that is always (safely) off that requires user action to go to the on or occupied mode.

We can provide today motion sensors, photoelectric switches, sound sensors, door switches and hood sash switches that keep equipment in a reduced capacity mode until ready for use. By considering the lab always "off" that needs to be physically indexed to "on," what would otherwise be around the clock standby position *is* the normal lab operating mode. The application of this concept will soon be the norm, driven by energy use costs as overall energy usage in the country for all users becomes more clear and as the trend for automatic electronic monitoring of long-term experimentation occurs.

It is difficult, as engineers, to speculate on what the future may hold. We do know that today, technology exists that has not yet been applied to the R&D facility because of economics and user "cultural" perception. When we change the way users view the lab as an infinite once through-one way disposable environment, we will make the advances necessary to enhance the lab safety with continuously reduced energy expenditure.

Outlook for the Federal Laboratories

CHRISTOPHER T. HILL [a]

RAND
2100 M Street NW
Washington, DC 20037-1270

This paper is about where the federal laboratory system may be headed, some of the stresses on that system, and some of the issues underlying the current policy debate about its future.

FEDERAL LABORATORIES IN BRIEF

It is said that there are 726 federal laboratories, but, in fact, no one quite knows how many laboratories there are. The annual budget for the federal laboratories, broadly defined, is about $28 billion. This represents their total expenditures, including funds spent at the laboratories by laboratory personnel on laboratory activities, as well as several billion dollars passed through to contractors.

Several laboratories also serve as grant making agencies. In the case of the National Institutes of Health, for example, about 75% of its total budget of $8.3 billion is passed through to universities, primarily to schools of medicine and, to a much lesser extent, to schools of science and engineering and to private firms. NIH performs about $2 billion of research and development in its own facilities and passes through about $6.5 billion annually. NASA, which is almost the same size, has a research and development budget of $8.5 billion, of which it spends about $2.6 billion in its own laboratories and passes through $6 billion, largely to industrial contractors.

Only 50 to 75 of the 700 or so federal laboratories are of broad interest to the policy community in Washington. These include the 20-odd Department of Energy laboratories, three of which are primarily concerned with nuclear weapons: Los Alamos, Sandia, and Lawrence Livermore, as well as the DOE multiprogram laboratories: Oak Ridge and Argonne. The Department of Defense has around 70 to 80 laboratories of which perhaps 25 or 30 are of significant size. NASA has eight major laboratories. The National Institutes of Health according to one source has 16, although some would say it has

[a] Senior Policy Analyst, RAND. The views expressed herein are the author's.

just one that includes a number of sublaboratories. This difference of view indicates the difficulty of enumerating the laboratories precisely. The Commerce Department has 52 major laboratories, but most of those are in NOAA and deal with such topics as fisheries and coastal processes rather than industrial commerce. In the Commerce Department, the National Institute of Standards and Technology in Gaithersburg, the former National Bureau of Standards, is one of the rising stars of the whole system.

The Agriculture Department has more than 200 laboratories, but most of them are small, focused on specific crops, pests, or regional needs. USDA has so many in part for traditional "pork barrel" reasons and in part because agricultural research is necessarily highly localized. If you want to study the cotton boll weevil, you cannot do so very effectively in Minneapolis—you must be in cotton country. And if you want to study the Mediterranean fruit fly, you need to be in the Los Angeles area, not in New Jersey. By contrast, nuclear energy can be studied anywhere that the neighbors will let you do it.

In addition, there are laboratories for the Environmental Protection Agency, the Department of Transportation, the Veterans Administration, the Tennessee Valley Authority, and so on.

Some of the laboratories are quite large. Several laboratories in the federal system spend more than $1 billion annually at a single facility. Los Alamos, Sandia, Livermore, and the National Institutes of Health are in that size range. They have thousands of employees and hundreds of buildings and other facilities.

STRESSES ON THE FEDERAL LABORATORIES

The federal laboratory system is facing a diverse set of pressures. The most fundamental pressure arises from a profound change in the reasons the federal government supports the conduct of research and development.

Government has supported science primarily because of our collective anxiety about the continuing struggle with death, whether it be from war, disease, pestilence, starvation, or poison. It can be argued that these anxieties account for most of the federal involvement in research: war (the Department of Defense), disease (NIH, the National Institutes of Mental Health, the Veterans Administration, and the Centers for Disease Control), pestilence and starvation (the Department of Agriculture), and poisoning (the Environmental Protection Agency, the National Institute of Occupational Safety and Health, the National Institute of Environmental Health Sciences). In fact, these five societal concerns account for most of the R&D spending. They also provide much of the rationale for continuing long-term support of fundamental research, a fact that is not always acknowledged in Washington.

Substantially fewer resources have been provided for R&D in support of other national goals. There has been a little bit for curiosity-driven research in astronomy, particle physics, and fundamental biology. And, there has been a small but rapidly growing pool of funds for research concerned with the more prosaic business of living well, through research to support a growing economy and rising production and consumption.

Members of Congress sometimes support R&D funding for personal reasons. It is sometimes said that Congress funds NIH so generously because its members want to live and serve forever, and because the best hope they have to do so is the research supported by NIH. Senator Dole's recent diagnosis of prostate cancer created much interest in research in that disease among the members. Members who are veterans of World War II remember too well how unprepared the United States was to fight determined vicious enemies on two fronts. They vow that we will never be caught unprepared again, and their experience tells them we must win by virtue of technological supremacy, so the nation spends $40 billion annually on research and development for national security.

High federal budget deficits are now squeezing the R&D budgets of all the federal agencies, leading to demands to reduce expenditures in the federal laboratories. While not all the laboratories are staffed by federal employees, they are not exempt from the sense that we ought to reduce the number of people on the public payroll. Furthermore, as the overall federal research and development budget shrinks, particularly on the national security side, there are demands to shift funds from the laboratories and into universities and industry on the grounds that we no longer need large weapons laboratories. Universities are quick to claim that they can spend federal R&D funds more efficiently than the laboratories. Similarly, the growth of corporate farming has tended to reduce the need for the network of small agriculture laboratories.

Recently, the federal laboratory system has not grown much, and existing facilities are becoming obsolete. The federal laboratory system grew rapidly during World War II with the growth of the national defense laboratories and of the nuclear weapons and other energy laboratories. There was additional major growth in the 60s and some growth in the 80s. However, there is unlikely to be much expansion of the laboratory system in the current decade.

Many of the laboratories have a new mission—to clean up after themselves. The DOD and DOE weapons laboratories operated for many years under an umbrella of protection from outside supervision, including from Congress, and they have a horrendous clean-up problem. It has been estimated that it may cost $200 to $300 billion to clean up after the laboratories, and some say that some of the messes created at the laboratories cannot be cleaned up at any price. From a laboratory director's point of view, environmental clean-up is a growth industry: cleaning up after ourselves can be seen as just as worthwhile as anything else the laboratories might do to help preserve our little low-entropy corner of the universe. Nevertheless, waste management is not quite as inspiring as the struggle for national survival that the laboratories have helped wage over the past several decades.

Another response to the changed conditions has been a new focus on competitiveness—on trying to use the laboratories to help our economic system create jobs, improve productivity, and strengthen industry. This trend has been helped by the campaign that the major research universities waged in the 1980s to convince Congress that funding research to be done in a particular place would make that place wealthy as a result. The scientific community has been very effective in selling this story to political leaders. This has, I believe, contributed to both the growth of research parks and the rapid emergence of "pork-barrel science." I also believe that the great interest in building new research facilities is based on a somewhat faulty interpretation of the successes of places like Silicon Valley, Route 128, and Research Triangle Park. Their success has depended on a great deal more than the concentration of research funding in these places.

Before about 1980, it was generally viewed as illegitimate for a federal laboratory to try to help its local region. However, the Stevenson Wydler Technology Innovation Act of 1980, the Federal Technology Transfer Act of 1986, the National Laboratory Technology Competitiveness Act of 1989, and other legislation have codified a set of new ideas about the proper relationship of laboratories to local and regional economic industrial activity. Before these acts were passed, it was acceptable for a laboratory to host a science fair or to encourage local school children to study math, but the notion that a laboratory's facilities could be used by a local machine shop, foundry, or biotech start-up company, and the notion that a federal laboratory employee could personally benefit from the work that he or she did in the laboratory, were totally unacceptable. In fact, such activities were generally viewed as contrary to the public interest.

Attitudes changed during the late 1970s and early 1980s as it was realized that to get something useful out of the research done in federal laboratories, it is important to let individuals and organizations benefit from their work. It was realized that research that belongs to everyone is often used by no one and that it was therefore useful to mobilize private gain and personal improvement in order to exploit the results more effectively. Consequently, mechanisms were established to allow companies to use laboratory facilities and to allow laboratory researchers to patent the results of their work or to share in the royalties from patents held by the government that are based on it. Federal laboratory employees could even start up a company on the outside and take with them patent rights that had been developed in the course of their federally sponsored research at the laboratory.

One result of this change has been, among other things, the growth of the "CRADA" process. A Cooperative Research and Development Agreement (a "CRADA") is a legal agreement between a federal laboratory and one or more companies that enables laboratory and corporate personnel to work together on research that is of interest to both the laboratory and the corporation. Typically, no funds pass between the laboratory and the companies. Rather, a CRADA is an agreement to work together, to exchange people and ideas, and to incorporate proper safeguards and protections for the intellectual property that might result or that is brought into the arrangement by the companies.

Several thousand such formal agreements between companies and laboratories have been developed over the last several years. This development is widely viewed with both enthusiasm and alarm. There is great enthusiasm because the laboratories are serving industry in new and important ways. The alarm has to do with the potential loss of focus on the laboratories' traditional missions. To illustrate, suppose we were to set up a new laboratory in rural New Mexico, hire 20,000 people to staff it, and direct them to invent nuclear weapons so as to make the world safe for democracy. Would we then want those same people to spend two days a week developing better ways of welding steam boilers? In other words, is it always in the national interest to divert scarce technical resources from a primary public mission such as space exploration, preservation of national security, or conservation of public health so that they can work on relatively mundane economic tasks instead? If we are in a cold war, the answer may well be no. However, under present circumstances, the answer is probably yes, at least to some extent. At the present time, the key issue has to do not with whether, but with how much of such activity is appropriate, as discussed below.

Each of the federal laboratories is organized under the aegis of a single federal agency. Implementation of CRADAs surely means a lessening of agency control over the laboratory's agenda. For example, the Department of Energy may be pursuing important national objectives through the large national energy laboratories. If laboratory personnel are busy doing commercial technology development deals, then they may not be available to work on the mission-oriented research that the Department needs. Such loss of agency direction and control is troubling to some thoughtful students of the CRADA process.

Industry has also occasionally been disappointed with the CRADA process. It often does not work well—it can be a bureaucratic nightmare, and implementation can take a long time. There are problems with allocation of intellectual property rights, and numerous other issues have come up. The laboratories have tended to oversell the CRADA opportunity, in part, because it is a survival strategy for them. Some saw their old missions withering away and have enthusiastically reached out to the CRADA mechanism as a way of trying to preserve jobs in the laboratory. Since some laboratories oversold what they were able to produce, some companies have entered into deals only to be disappointed with their results. (I should note that useful results have also come out of these arrangements.)

To an extent, working with industry is a survival strategy for federal laboratories—a way to broaden their constituencies. However, it is one thing for a laboratory in a region to have a highly specialized and focused constituency; it is another to be able to help build the economy of an entire region. The latter multiplies the number of local officials and others who would like to see each laboratory maintain its budget. Some of the states have led in building political support for the laboratories because they have had greater commitment to research and development or because the federal presence has been more important to the state's economy. For example, New Mexico, which is the home of Los Alamos, Sandia, White Sands, and other smaller facilities, has been a leader. More than 10 percent of the gross state product of New Mexico arises directly from research and development; a percentage that is much greater than in states like New Jersey, Massachusetts, California, and Maryland, which are usually thought of as R&D-intensive states. R&D spending in New Mexico amounts to $2.5 billion annually, of which $2.3 billion is spent in two large weapons laboratories, Los Alamos and Sandia. It should be no surprise, then, that the two senators from New Mexico have led the national policy debate on the future of the federal laboratories: the future well-being of New Mexico is at stake.

WHITHER THE FEDERAL LABORATORIES?

Whether CRADAs can "save" the federal laboratories is part of the larger political issue of what to do with the laboratories in the future. Like military bases, even if they have outlived their usefulness, laboratories—especially large ones—are not likely to be shut down. Recently, respected studies by the Office of Technology Assessment, the Center for Strategic and International Studies, and the private sector Council on Competitiveness have examined new and different ways to manage the federal laboratory resources.

President Clinton seems to support the laboratories in his technology policy and science policy statements. For example, in May 1993, he gave a stirring speech at Los Alamos High School about the past contributions of the laboratories and about his expectations for the future. He was interrupted by applause many times, reflecting the fact that he was talking about sustaining Los Alamos National Laboratory by giving it new missions to meet new national challenges. However, this view has not yet been articulated in a new federal budget, so we do not know where he is going to come out on funding.

Two bills introduced in Congress in spring 1993 address the future of the laboratories. Because they were introduced by leading members and because they differ substantially in content and intent, they warrant serious attention.

Congressman George Brown, a representative from California who chairs the House Committee on Science, Space, and Technology and, by virtue of that, oversees a substantial fraction of the laboratories' efforts, introduced the Department of Energy Laboratory Technology Act. Paraphrasing, it would tell the Energy Department: do not diversify so much, keep your nonmission research below 10% of the total, establish a commission to consider laboratory consolidation, and create a new organizational structure in the office of the Secretary of Energy to exert strategic direction over the laboratories for the first time since DOE was created. This bill mandates that the Energy Department handle the CRADA process more efficiently than it now does. It also creates a commission to be established under the Federal Coordinating Council on Science, Engineering, and Technology to study the possibility of long-term reorganization and even closure of some federal laboratories, not limited to the energy laboratories.

The Brown bill is viewed with dismay by some in the laboratory community. However, Brown is looking to the future by putting some very hard questions on the table.

The Senate bill, introduced by Senator Bennett Johnston of Louisiana, is called the Department of Energy National Cooperative Technologies Partnership Act. Senator Johnston chairs both the authorizing committee and the appropriations subcommittee that influence the Energy Department's laboratories. The Johnston bill takes a different approach from the Brown bill. It would tell the laboratories to build up partnerships with industry and to spend at least 10% of each laboratory's resources on cooperative partnerships with industry. Whereas Representative Brown's bill sets a cap of 10% on such activities, Senator Johnston's bill sets a 10% floor. Johnston's bill directs the laboratories to focus their research on the critical technologies identified by the National Critical Technologies Panel. It also tells the Energy Department to manage its CRADAs more efficiently. While it includes a number of other housekeeping measures, it says nothing at all about laboratory consolidation or closure.

In summary, the Johnston bill appears to be expansionist and focused on laboratory diversification, while the Brown bill looks to a possible reduction in the size of the federal laboratory system and to a sharper laboratory focus on agency missions. Thus the fundamental issue for the laboratories in the next 5-10 years, assuming that nothing of major proportion occurs to cause them to move in yet another direction, is whether to consolidate, focus, and close some laboratories, or to diversify, activate, and expand the federal laboratory system. This question is likely to be addressed by the Administration when it puts its fiscal 1995 budget proposal on the table in January 1994.

It is important to note that the Department of Defense is closing laboratories now. A number of DOD's laboratories are located on military bases, and some of these are likely to be closed as their host bases are closed as a result of decisions recommended by the base-closing commission.

In contrast to most other laboratories, the National Institute of Standards and Technology is currently undergoing rapid expansion. It just received about $60 million for new physical facilities in Gaithersburg, and its budget for external research support is slated to increase very rapidly.

Construction has begun in Texas on the superconducting super collider, which will be the largest laboratory and one of the largest concrete structures ever built.[b] We may see an expansion of the Environmental Protection Agency's research facilities. Most other departments' laboratories, including those at NIH, appear unlikely to grow.

[b] In October 1993, Congress terminated all funding for the superconducting super collider except that needed to effect an orderly close-out of this unfinished project.

Critique by Roundtable

The Future Outlook—Some Speculations About the Lab of the Future

Participants were the morning speakers (Baker, French, Stark) and Dennis Flannagan, Robert McGhee, and construction manager and architect Norberte Young, Jr. The discussions were moderated by Dr. Alice Huang.

AMENITY AS A NECESSITY FOR INTERACTION

The participants addressed the need for amenities and the inherent trade-offs. Different ways to configure space to promote interaction both in terms of office placement and size and in design of break areas were discussed. It was generally agreed that not enough thought is given to the design of staircases and elevators. Dr. Williamson emphasized the importance of stairs for interaction as well as being a device for overcoming the inconvenience of waiting. This led to a discussion of the tradeoffs between space requirements for a staircase designed as a public gathering place and their cost in reduced net-to-gross ratios. There were reminders as well for the need in setting priorities, for a program advocate or champion to preserve the amenities of the building by ensuring that they are included in the planning process, and then by seeing that they are not converted into further lab space.

THE IMPORTANCE OF OFFICES IN SUPPORTING INTERACTION

Dr. Huang identified offices as a primary interaction area for scientists. Observers from the audience noted that desk locations for graduate students and junior faculty in nonhierarchical areas is critical to achieve interaction.

Stark noted that one option may be the kind of open office space apart from the lab that appeared in the "office papoose" scheme.

McGhee noted that as we push the lab desk further from the labs, we alter the interactions historically associated with lab science. This distancing may be more difficult to achieve in academia than in corporate facilities.

SALK: BACK TO THE FUTURE

Norberte Young noted how he was struck by the constant references to Salk. He wondered even though it is 30 years old, whether it is a prototype for the future.

McGhee acknowledged that it is a prototype. Its flexibility is derived from the 16,000 sf open floor plate served by an interstitial floor. He noted that a lot of lab buildings work as well or better, but it is a basepoint for design.

It is commanding and inspiring because it is a place of quality to house science. As a result, it elevates the conduct of the process of science.

CONTROLS AND THEIR LIMITS

The amount of air handling that will be required in a facility and ways to individualize control within a function or space within a facility were also addressed in some detail with Mr. Baker and Mr. French offering successful examples of local cooling. This led to discussion of the complexity resulting from providing increased variability, through sophisticated control systems, which creates problems for users and for maintenance staff. Again, organization lags behind technology.

A participant from the audience suggested that since instrumentation is key in driving the ratio of support to laboratory, the instrument designers and manufacturers might be brought into the dialogue to discuss how the instruments can be redesigned in terms of heat generation.

Mr. Baker suggested that simply advising the engineering team about which would be wet labs and which would be dry labs would enable the research and development organization to take advantage of the difference in cost.

MORE RESPONSES TO FLEXIBILITY

An audience member suggested that instead of running utilities every place, we should provide interstitial floors so utilities can be dropped quickly just to where we need them.

French requested a better definition of flexibility requirements 10 years out.

Huang countered in favor of looser, more forgiving floor plate patterns of space.

DEALING WITH THE HIDDEN CONSTITUENCIES

It was generally agreed that instrumentation, fume hoods, controls, and lab furniture help drive the costs of research facilities. Yet, as industries, they lack dialogue with one another. A key question that arose from the discussion was how to develop the clout to engage them as participants in the design process. The full force of all parties involved is needed to get better design, and coordination between the manufacturers of fume hoods, controls, lab furniture, and instrumentations. Architects and engineers have had some impact, but they are not a large enough constituency on their own to command attention from a fragmented industry. It will take the National Institutes of Health, corporate users, and major universities using their market clout to lead the way. We are all in this together.

Roundtable Discussion

Participants were Timothy Baker, Stanley Stark, Christopher Hill, and Leon Lewis along with members of the audience. Dr. Huang moderated.

THE FEDERAL LABS

There was a discussion of the need to share facilities more as a way of gaining greater efficiency while managing the challenge of cultural differences. The Federal labs are reaching out to what might become their natural constituency–research-oriented universities that could use their Federal resources to help conduct some of their work, but there is a degree of competition between universities and federal labs for federal research dollars. In a discussion of ways in which former weapons labs are finding a way to participate meaningfully in the national economy, it was revealed that they are vigorously pursuing interaction with industry, the auto industry, in particular, which is putting up a great deal of money for cooperative research with those labs.

There was speculation that in view of anticipated cutbacks in funding for federal labs, there is not likely to be new funding for new labs; the emphasis will be on retrofitting.

AMENITY

Issues of the appearance and amenities in the lab surfaced again, with frustration expressed regarding the lack of recreational facilities, particularly in the corporate environment. Use of a building's roof for recreation was proposed as a low-cost alternative, and "fun" environments within and around the building, such as art programs, were suggested to address the problem of sameness without significantly increasing the budget.

MAINTENANCE AND ECONOMY

A discussion of problems resulting from insufficient funds for building maintenance, and even for safety, focused on the need for top-down strategic decision making to allot funds within the research organization. The participants stressed a need for commitment at the top to set aside funds to restore, renovate, expand, and improve facilities. It was acknowledged that preventative maintenance is critical and that deferred maintenance only intensifies the problem. The development of models for dealing with this overwhelming problem will help achieve efficiency. Computer maintenance packages are now on the market, and there is even a full course of study on research and development facility maintenance at the University of Wisconsin.

Dr. Lewis stressed that the life of a building depends on aggressive commitment to a maintenance and replacement program.

Troubled by the increasing complexity of maintenance systems, a speaker in the audience advocated the principle of KISS (keep it simple, stupid) in order to spend less of one's budget on complex "toys" that break down. Mr. Stark replied by stressing the need to do serious total life cycle cost analysis–of which maintenance is a part.

Another speaker from the floor commented that in view of the uncertainty of the economy, one cannot really plan budget maintenance in life cycle costs, which is all the more reason to keep it simple. Making it simple so maintenance costs are simple all along minimizes the worry about what happens when the budget gets cut.

An audience participant added that it costs too much money in down time not to be addressing the maintenance crisis, wherein, for instance, a scientists often cannot conduct an experiment because chilled water is not available to cool the laser.

Finally, and rather grimly, a number of audience members suggested as an antidote to trying to fight obsolescence by overspending on construction costs, accept obsolescence and a short building life span. Their belief was that this would result in less expensive components, systems, finishes, and no additional incremental investment in either durability or flexibility.

[**Editor's note:** No one volunteered to be the first to test the merit of this provocative suggestion for their next facility.]

Concluding Remarks

STANLEY STARK

Haines Lundberg Waehler
115 Fifth Avenue
New York, New York 10003

This Workshop had many insightful and revealing moments. Its great strength was the diversity of viewpoints which revealed many significant possibilities and issues for the Lab of the Future. A consensus developed around some major conclusions:

- Given the dramatic impact rapidly changing equipment and instrumentation have on lab layout and research operations, a closer alliance is required between manufacturers of equipment and lab furniture, scientists, facility planners, and designers.

- More evaluation and scrutiny of costs are required. There should be more evaluation of the life cycle costs of design alternatives. There was also some feeling that certain kinds of obsolescence should be accepted as a method of avoiding excessive costs.

- The advantages of technically sophisticated building systems must be weighed against the operating and maintenance costs these systems impose to be certain that during the life of the facility, the resources are there to sustain their operations.

- Layout and building designs should be tested by multiple occupancy scenarios before design finalization.

- How research is conducted is changing due to the pressures of competitiveness, increased speed, and funding reductions. It is this change in style and operating approach that, more than any other set of forces, will drive how research facilities must change in the future.

The discussions that began at this Workshop must be continued among colleagues and peers. Continuous scrutiny and active anticipation will permit us to get in front of the wave of change, but only if we can maintain the discipline and the commitment to continue to look forward.

Our hope is that the audience of the Workshop and the readers of these *Annals* have drawn the insight and the sustenance to continue these dialogues. The future is empty; it is waiting. It is both our responsibility and our great opportunity to define it.

Index of Contributors